GRIEF HEALING:

A Doctor's Excruciating Experience [Through the Incredible Life of His Wife Sylvia]

Dr John M Gullo

Clinical Psychologist

Interior Graphics/Art Credit: Dr John M Gullo

Balboa Press books may be ordered through booksellers or by contacting:

Balboa Press
A Division of Hay House
1663 Liberty Drive
Bloomington, IN 47403
www.balboapress.com
1 (877) 407-4847

Print information available on the last page.

ISBN: 978-1-5043-6343-3 (sc)
ISBN: 978-1-5043-6344-0 (e)

Library of Congress Control Number: 2016912423

Balboa Press rev. date: 08/11/2016

Table of Contents

DEDICATION

THIS WRITING IS DEDICATED to the memory of my beloved wife **Sylvia**. A 51 year relationship with an **amazing woman of remarkable breathtaking talent and a cornucopia of skills.** Sylvia was born on August 27, 1936. She passed away, untimely, on April 7, 2015 at the age of 78. Sylvia Loreen is a woman who **enriched my life immeasurably!** In a word: **HyperWife!!!** Which is greater, more superior than "Super"- or "Ultra-". The **Zenith!**

ACKNOWLEDGEMENTS

Thank You...

To MY DAUGHTER Sylvia Loreen Gullo, II and my sister Bernadette Mary Gullo McCoy who, independently within days of each other, both suggested that I write a book - not necessarily this book. I am grateful to both of them for their suggestion, request and encouragement.

INTRODUCTION

MENTAL CONSTIPATION CAME initially. Then, after rearranging my mental furniture (sometimes called "soul –searching"), I had an epiphany wherein I unearthed a three-fold responsibility to author this book.

My first and foremost obligation is to pay tribute to my wife Sylvia L. Gullo. For me to be a **Warrior Ambassador.**

An **Ambassador** is the highest ranking (or special) representative of another person. There can only be one ambassador in a marriage: The **spouse**. No one else **possesses the knowledge** to be the ambassador. So, all others are relegated to being a spokesperson. If both spouses expire simultaneously, there is no ambassador. Only spokespersons remain.

My second duty for authoring this book is to provide my wife Sylvia's entire family with who Sylvia really is/was. Sylvia's family deserves to know a lot more about her. I'm eager to be the only knowledgeable guide on this somewhat tortuous but amazing journey.

The third reason is an attempt to assist others in following a proven pathway to grief healing thru my poignant experience in the untimely passing of my beloved wife Sylvia. If someone requires your help, usually you have an obligation to help them.

Having practiced Clinical Psychology, Psychotherapy and Medical Hypnosis for over 50 years, I discovered one of the better methods to assist others in their recovery from emotional pain was thru self-disclosure whenever possible. I believe that anytime you are exposed to a personal story, it tends to resonate well. An experience with which you can connect.

So with that in mind, I first want to chronicle my deeply personal experience with my wife. Naturally, in my view (which is the only one that counts!), Sylvia is the Greatest Woman to have ever walked on planet earth!!! Solutions I provide subsequently.

Your experience(s) may be vastly different from mine. I promise you, you'll discover benefits. You won't be disappointed.

Grief

Grief is usually associated with the death of a spouse, parent(s) or child(ren). It could include other relatives or friends that feel like family. Pets qualify.

Depression is a synonym for grief. However, depression is more often associated with one's own behavior (e.g. failure). For me, I consider grief as a severe degree of depression related **only to the loss of human (in some cases pet) life.**

Does it make any difference? Is the distinction important? Yes. Why? Because grief recovery requires a somewhat different set of thoughts. A different mind set. An in-your-face confrontation with mortality.

Most people start entertaining mortality in their 40's. Mid life crisis. But it can start as early as age 30.

Ask someone when they think they are going to die. Or, how long they expect to live. The body accommodates. The actual physical degradation begins halfway to their stated age of death. So, if the answer is they expect to live to or die at age 98, then at age 49 their body begins the gradual death process.

Who in the hell likes to think about death? Who wants to prepare themselves for the loss of a loved one? Virtually no one.

As painful as it might be, prepping yourself can mitigate the depths of grief. And, the time it takes to heal. It's probably to late for the vast majority of the readers of this book to profit from this advanced planning. But, it's not too late for you too help others. Does that mean you are your brothers' keeper? Well, why not? Your choice. Make it right so you can live by the "light"

My goal in creating this book is not to just nibble at the edges of grief. I'm going for the "heart".

Trust me on this. It's much easier to spend 10 hours reading this book rather than 10 years of miseries caused by your own ignorance. Not to mention perilous thinking.

Young girl growing up

Wedding Reception

Honeymoon, Washington, DC

On Vacation

Preparing For Evening Out

Las Vegas Vacation

Chapter

Author's Life From Birth To Early Marriage

I was born on July 28, 1938 in Springfield, Illinois. As I write this, March 2016, I am 77 years old. My Father, Jasper Scime Gullo was an Attorney-at-Law and first generation Scilian (Italian) American. His parents immigrated to the United States early in 1911. His mother, my grandmother, was pregnant with my father on the boat to New York from Sicily. My father had a younger brother and sister (who was the youngest).

My mother, Esther Elizabeth Murphy, was a homemaker. Her mother was of German descent (Schwab). And, her father was, obviously, of Irish descent.

I was named John Marshall. My father was of major influence in naming me. First "John" was his father's name which he wanted to honor. Second, "Marshall" was the last name of the 13th Supreme Court Justice of the United States: John Marshall, who lived from 1755 to 1835 and served as Chief Justice from 1801 to 1835 when he died. It was coincidental that both men had the same first name.

Subsequently, my parents had three more boys, I being the eldest. The first males were all born in July: the 28th, the 7th and the 11th. Finally, the fifth and last child born was my sister Bernadette Mary who is a Respiratory Therapist. The third child, my Social Worker brother Donald, drowned at the age of 29. The exact same age of our maternal uncle who was killed in an auto wreck with a train several years earlier. The second male child, my brother Robert, is a Plumbing, Heating and Air conditioning contractor. My youngest brother Dennis, the fourth child, is an Electrician.

I never really knew my maternal grandparents because they died before I was able to get to know them. My mother was the 5th of 9 children. There were 5 girls and 4 boys.

Up until around 4 years old I spent a lot of time with my paternal grandparents and was bilingual (Italian and English). Subsequently, however, I lost that language skill as my father did not want to teach me Italian. Why? Because he, being Italian, was discriminated against growing up. He shined shoes to make money to obtain a Law education and experienced prejudice in that capacity.

I attended Blessed Sacrament parochial grade school. In kindergarten I had some trouble learning as well as walking as I stumbled and fell down a lot. The cause? I needed corrective eye glasses. Once I got the eye glasses I no longer had trouble walking. The learning part, as I determined retroactively, had a monumental impact in that I never acquired a love for reading. I had no trouble reading. But, not liking to read that much, it was a chore. Looking back, it was pure driven desire that allowed me to overcome the reading issue to attain a doctoral degree.

Some early experiences in my life were fortuitous in that they became invaluable as an adult (more on this in Chapter 7, Caregiving). Around the age of 6 I was interested in cooking and learned a lot from my Grandmother, Aunt and my Mother. At age 10 or 11 in the fifth grade, I rode my bicycle from school to home to prepare lunch for my mother who was recovering from an illness.

Being the oldest child, I was expected to help my mother with domestic chores. Consequently I learned how to wash clothes with a ringer washer, dry clothes on a clothes line, and iron clothes with both a hand iron and mangle ironing board. A mangle was an electrically operated roller used to press (iron) sheets and other clothing. I also learned how to sew and darn socks using a light bulb inserted in the sock in order to have a solid surface to sew the sock hole together. Of course I learned how to clean house and all other domestic duties. At the age of 10, I also helped my mother change diapers and bottle feed by youngest brother. Subsequently, I did the same for my sister who was 12 years my junior.

Some of my maternal male relatives were employed in the construction business as carpenters, painters, plasterers, concrete and brick-laying, house framing, and roofing to name a few. So, my exposure to these trades benefited me as well.

I then attended a public high school for the first semester of my freshman year. That was unsatisfying to me. Back in those days Parochial schools were usually better sources of education because of the powerful dedication of the nuns, brothers and priests. Thus, I enrolled in the catholic Cathedral Boys High School which was taught by the Viatorian Brothers and Priests. That Order is no longer in existence. In 1956 I graduated from this high school at the top tier of my class.

My plans were to become a Medical Doctor specifically an Obstetrician and Gynecologist.

I had an academic scholarship to attend the University of Illinois in Champaign/Urbana which was 90 miles from my home in Springfield, Illinois. I only went to the Univ. of Illinois for the first semester. It was way to large of an Institution for my liking. For the second semester, I transferred to my hometown Springfield Junior College which was a catholic school. That proved to be a much better experience partly because it was much smaller and more intimate. I had the opportunity to take one course that had a potent impact and indelible influence on the rest of my academic and professional life: Logic. Logic is not hardly taught anymore in higher education. I believe Logic is the single most important course above all others. In my opinion, Logic would best be a mandated course in College. If there were only one academic course available it 'should' be Logic. Knowledge of logic is indispensible! Logic is a precursor to the scientific method. Knowing a logical thought process mitigates a plethora of perilous issues. I will discuss this in more detail later.

For my sophomore (second) year of college I went to MacMurray College in Jacksonville, Illinois, a city 25 miles to the west. Up until that time, 1957, MacMurray was an all girls College. I was one of about 12 male sophomores along with about 80 freshman males and over 300 female students in all four years of their education. That was an experience extraordinaire for conspicuous reasons.

As a senior in college I became friends with a Clinical Psychology M.A. Graduate student Robert Matirko. We remain friends to this day and Dr. Robert Matirko lives and practices in Los Angeles, California. Accidentally, we both recognized that we had a mutual interest in Hypnosis. I knew of an M.D. Psychiatrist in my hometown of Springfield (half hour drive from college) who used hypnosis in his practice and taught a hypnosis course. Consequently, I arranged for the both of us and 4 other Graduate Clinical Psychology students to take this hypnosis course. That was the genesis of my sub career in Medical Hypnosis.

I helped my friend Robert Matirko by typing his Personality and Intellectual and Neuropsychological evaluations, for which I was paid. [Neuropsychological evaluation consists of various tests of cognitive, motor, and perceptual skills that are sensitive to brain functioning problems.] At that time Robert administered an I.Q. (Intelligence Quotient) test to me. The results placed me in the top category of Very Superior. Having this exposure and experience in helping Robert with his Clinical Psychology education definitely gave me an advantage when I studied for the same college degree.

I graduated from MacMurray College with a Bachelor of Arts (B.A.) degree in 1961 as a pre-med major in chemistry as well as psychology. Since MacMurray didn't accept all of my prior college credits, I had to attend another (9th) semester (4.5 years). The courses available during the times I wanted were all in psychology. I had an interview with a medical school in Illinois in 1970. However, after my exposure to the psychology courses, I thought that might be interesting to pursue immediately instead of having to wait another year to go to medical school. So, I actually got into the psychology field by accident.

I then attended Bradley University in Peoria, Illinois. In 1962 I graduated from Bradley with a Masters of Arts (M.A.) degree in clinical psychology.

In the Fall of 1962 I began a one-year clinical psychology internship at the Jacksonville (Illinois) State Mental Hospital. My duties included extensive psychological testing which involved Personality, Intellectual and, Neuropsychological assessments. I also had to provide individual and group psychotherapy. And, I participated in multi professional diagnostic, progress, and discharge team meetings. Upon successful completion of this internship, I was invited to continue my employment as a Psychologist I, which I did. The duties remained the same but with autonomy and also provided supervision for interns. I held that position for one year and was promoted to Psychologist II. One year later, 1965 I was again promoted to Psychologist III. Once again, the duties remained the same but with added supervisory responsibilities. And, I was in charge of an alcoholic and drug abuse treatment program as well as a consultant to a County substance abuse program. [The highest clinical psychologist position was a Psychologist V. There was only one Psychologist V who was the State's Head Psychologist. In 1969, I was again promoted. This time I became a Psychologist IV.

After I completed my internship in the Fall of 1963, I and three other colleagues began a part-time clinical psychology private practice. Independently, I became a psychological testing (Personality and Intelligence/Neuropsychological) consultant for a Group Psychiatry practice. That consultant relationship continued until 1979 when we moved to Florida. The part-time Psychotherapy practice prevailed until 1975 when I resigned from the Illinois Department of Mental Health and went into a Full Time private practice.

In 1962 my friend Robert Matirko sent me some professional articles written by the soon-to-be internationally famous New York City clinical psychologist Dr. Albert Ellis, Ph.D. Dr. Ellis created a whole new system of Psychotherapy that emphasized logic and reason. Earlier, you recall, I emphasized the importance of a college course in Logic. I was naturally compelled to adopt and participate in the development of this system. Originally it was called Rational Therapy (RT). Then the system name was changed to Rational-Emotive Therapy (RET), followed by Rational-Emotive Behavior Therapy (REBT for the lip-weary).

The best way to explain Rational-Emotive behavior Therapy is to quote the Albert Ellis Institute's website description. "…the **Albert Ellis Institute (AEI),** a world renowned psychotherapy training Institute established in 1959. AEI is committed to promoting emotional well-being through the research and application of effective, short-term therapy with long-term results. AEI's therapeutic approach is based on rational emotive behavior therapy (REBT), the pioneering form of cognitive behavior therapy. **REBT** is an action-oriented Psychotherapy that teaches individuals to identify, challenge, and replace their self-defeating beliefs with healthier ones that promote emotional well-being and goal achievement. REBT was developed in 1955 by Dr. Albert Ellis. Dr. Ellis has been considered one of the most influential psychotherapists in history. In a survey conducted in 1982 among approximately 800 American clinical and counseling psychologists, Albert Ellis was considered even more influential in the field than Sigmund Freud. Prior to his death in 2007 (September 27, 2007 at age 93. Added by me), Psychology Today described him as the 'greatest living psychologist.'…REBT (is) one of the most widely practiced forms of psychotherapy in the World."

REBT is evidence-based, heavily involved in research and publishes it's own **Journal of Cognitive and Behavioral Psychotherapies** formerly known as the **Journal of Rational Emotive and Cognitive Behavior Therapy** (prior to 2013).

Dr. Albert Ellis served as an associate or consulting editor of a plethora of scientific journals. A prolific writer, Dr. Ellis published over 700 scientific papers and more than 150 audio and video cassette tapes. He has authored or edited over 60 books and monographs most of which were best-selling popular and professional volumes.

Perhaps, Dr. Ellis most seminal writing was ***A Guide to Rational Living*** (co-authored by his clinical psychologist colleague Dr. Robert

A. Harper, Ph.D.), which was published in 1961. That is now known as the Original ***A Guide to Rational Living.***

A second, revised edition was published in 1975 and titled ***A New Guide to Rational Living.*** On page 202 of the first paragraph of Chapter 21 of this 2nd edition (RATIONAL-EMOTIVE THERAPY OR RATIONNAL BEHAVIORAL TRAINING UPDATED), Dr. Ellis says "…RET has gone through many minor and some major changes, originated by myself and some of my main collaborators over the years – especially Dr. Robert A. Harper, Dr. H. Jon Geis, Edward Garcia, Dr. William Knaus, **Dr. John M. Gullo……"**

The third edition of this book was released in 1997 and was titled the same as the original: ***A Guide To Rational Living.***

Prior to Dr. Ellis 1975 acknowledgement of me as one of his main collaborators in the development of Rational Emotive Behavior Therapy, he and I co-authored the book ***Murder and Assassination*** published in 1971. Also in that same year (1971), I authored a chapter in Dr. Ellis' book ***Growth Through Reason.*** Before that (1963) I wrote a book review of Dr. Ellis" book ***Reason and Emotion in Psychotherapy*** for a Journal of the American Psychological Association.

I can tell you, unequivocally, that both Dr. Albert Ellis and I, were/are mavericks. Actually, hardcore mavericks!

The State of Illinois from around the 1950's through the 1980's provided advanced degree subsidization for those Master's Level clinical psychologists that were qualified. All college tuition and expenses along with money for room and board was paid for by the State of Illinois. Thus, in the Fall of 1965 I was enrolled in a doctoral psychology program. However, that doctoral program was discontinued after 1 semester. I then resumed my work with the Jacksonville (IL) State Hospital.

In 1975 I finally obtained my doctoral degree in clinical psychology from the University of Sarasota. Subsequently, The University of Sarasota became known as Argosy University with campuses in both Sarasota and Tampa, Florida. Argosy University only provides education for advanced degrees in Clinical Psychology and some other fields as well.

CHAPTER

AUTHOR'S WIFE'S LIFE FROM BIRTH UNTIL COURTSHIP

THE YEAR WAS 1936. The date was August 27th. And Sylvia Loreen Beckman was born in Denver, Colorado. [She was 2 years older than me. And, at 5'6", she was 2 inches taller than me.]

Sylvia's father was William Beckman, and her mother was Ruth Jones Beckman. Sylvia was the oldest of 5 children. She had 4 brothers. However, the youngest brothers were twins but only one survived. Most of Sylvia's father's family resided in Denver. One uncle migrated to Peoria, Illinois. A town 60 miles north of Jacksonville and Springfield, Illinois. Sylva's parents did not stay in Denver for long. They moved to the Jacksonville, Illinois area not long after Sylvia was born. This is where most of her mother's family lived.

Sadly, Sylvia grew up in severe poverty. Her father had an alcohol problem. [Were this fact not common knowledge, I wouldn't even be noting it.] Thus, there were limited financial resources for food. She was constantly scavenging for food in others garbage cans. Sometimes she would find fruit, for example, only partially eaten, that she washed and ate. Her nutrition was so compromised that she did not get enough calcium to maintain any semblance of dental health. The result, she had to have what remained of her teeth removed as a young teenager and replaced with dentures.

Naturally, coming from such a despoiled background, she had inadequate and severely limited clothing. The inevitable consequence? She was made fun of at school. Oppressively insulted and hazed. Too, she was consistently picked last for any sports game. I mean, put yourself in her shoes and just try to imagine what it would be like for you to be so severely ostracized. I wouldn't even want that to happen to a pit bull dog. Most would be tempted to conclude that such unpropitious, adverse circumstances would spoliate (ruin) someone for life.

Making matter worse, Sylvia became a product of a broken home. Her parents divorced during her childhood.

At the age of 16 Sylvia became pregnant by a traveling musician. A short lived relationship with a man who never returned to her as promised. She was discriminated against medically at the time of birth delivery. Fortunately, the birth of her first child, a daughter (1953), was not compromised. In 1954/5 she got married and progenated 3 more children. A girl, a boy and another boy. [More about this relationship in a later Chapter.]

There's not much more for me to expound on about Sylvia's life before we met that would be relevant. Elaborating on Sylvia's gravely impoverished background is not necessary. I believe you get the point. Also, I could, with dexterity, embellish Sylvia's early life. But what the hell would be the point?

I want to take a break.

CHAPTER

LOVE AT FIRST SIGHT

IT WAS IN the early Spring of 1964. I walked into a special room to participate in a Psychiatric Team meeting (at the Jacksonville, IL State Mental Hospital). I sat down next to a beautiful woman whom I'd never seen before. I experienced an intangible powerful, obscure drive to connect with Sylvia. A strange, undefined and indescribable feeling flooded my body. In a word: smitten. I felt compelled to smile and initiate a conversation with Sylvia. Shortly, I gently placed my hand on her knee as a gesture of sincerity. Later I was able to recognize and identify that experience as "Love at first sight." Sylvia, I quickly found out, was a psychiatric technician.

Later on as the relationship began to develop, Sylvia admitted that she had similar feelings. Her initial reaction, she said, was that she didn't like me. But, she couldn't resist my advances. So, once again, "Love at first sight."

That initial encounter led to......

CHAPTER

COURTSHIP

WITHIN A FEW days, Sylvia and I had our first date in my Staff residence located on the grounds of the Jacksonville (IL) State Mental Hospital. We engaged in a nice and comfortable conversation for awhile initially. That was followed by an irresistible, overpowering intimate relationship. Mutually that was astonishingly gratifying. The electricity between us was enough to blow a commercial transformer. Smokin' hot comes to mind. And, a first for each of us.

That, my friends, is the genesis of a long-term relationship. For when we gazed into each others eyes we saw eternal love and devotion. I was 26 years old and not looking to get married.

It was during our second date that I learned that Sylvia was married and had 4 children aged 4 to 11. That fact had no negative impact on me.

Quickly, I found myself no longer trying to meet up with other ladies at lounges, bars and parties. I became progressively more satisfied with our evolving relationship.

Jacksonville, Illinois was a small community of 25,000 people. It only had, at that time 3 fine dining restaurants. I choose the Holiday

Inn (which back-in–the–day most franchises had excellent restaurants). It was sometime in June of 1964. So, Sylvia and I went to dinner. Shortly after being seated, Sylvia sheepishly inquired as to why there were two forks. I was jolted with my own insensitivity. A psychological embolism. Me, a psychologist trained to be sensitive, failed to recognize that Sylvia's destitute beginning disallowed her the knowledge of fine dining tableware placement and usage. Were I more cognizant, I could have remarked something like: "The smaller salad fork and the larger dinner fork (obviously **not** 'entre') were nice looking and properly placed". I vowed to myself right-then-and-there to not make that mistake again! We had one helluva great meal. A filet mignon for Sylvia, which she had never eaten before. And a filet mignon for me. She was very grateful! I, humorously remarked: "Get used to it, my love, as we're going to be doing this often."

In July of 1964 we went to a St Louis, Mo. Municipal Opera show. A married couple from India were our friends and accompanied us. The wife, Esther, was a psychologist colleague of mine at the State Hospital and her husband, Vijay, worked in another professional department of the Hospital. While visiting with this couple, Esther invited Sylvia and I to go with them of the St. Louis Muny Opera. Sylvia's eyes lit up like a powerful beam of light from the high noon Sun. I could tell that she yearned to see the opera. I was quite impressed with how much pleasure she derived from her off-the-scale dazzling experience.

We stayed at a Hotel overnight on this trip. It was at this hotel that I broke down weeping with joy the realization of how deeply in love I was with Sylvia. It was an issue I was dealing with for awhile. But love-at-first-sight is unrelenting and eventually smacks you in the face vanquishing any mental constipation!

In August of 1964 I flew to Los Angeles, California to attend an American Psychological Association Convention. There I purchased some fine jewelry for Sylvia. It was my first gift to her since our initial encounter about4 months earlier. When I gave Sylvia the jewelry, she was both awed and gladdened. It was quite notable to her having come from downtrodden roots.

Sylvia's husband's employment required that he be out-of-town frequently. Hence, our being together necessitated logistics planning.

Our relationship continued to grow and deepen.

As I noted earlier, I left Jacksonville, IL in the Fall of 1965 to pursue a State of Illinois subsidized doctoral degree in psychology. Since that doctoral program was being discontinued, I returned to Jacksonville, IL in January of 1966 to resume work with the State Mental Hospital.

Shortly after I returned, I proposed marriage. Sylvia was always fond of telling others that she gave me an ultimatum for marriage. Obviously, Sylvia excitedly accepted.

Now for the painful part...

As this story unfolds, you will see how onerous and gut-wrenching it is to talk about. Not long after my marriage proposal Sylvia confided in me a thorough run-down of her marriage situation. She did not divulge anything (nor did I ever ask) about her marriage earlier so as not to lead me to wrongly apprise her motivation.

She said the marriage was one of convenience as she was looking, at that time, for someone to help raise her very young daughter. She was still poverty-stricken and wanted to find some way to better provide for her daughter. Maternal love thrusts one into a position of being forced to make difficult decisions. While the love was absent, she thought she could make it work. Unfortunately, she was unaware of the serious problems her husband had. These difficulties emerged relatively soon in their marital relationship. She went on to say that he was an alcoholic and that she was subject to both physical and mental abuse. (Nowadays, we call this domestic abuse/violence). Not only did she fear for her own life, but she was fearful for her children's lives. Her husband's alcohol fueled outbursts were unpredictable and were progressively getting worse. Sylvia noted that she felt trapped and handcuffed in this relationship. You might say an emotional headlock. She had considerable chronic enmity. And, was down on herself for marrying an alcoholic exactly like her father (though he wasn't an abuser). Sylvia went on to say that her husband was not financially responsible in providing food and clothes for her 4 children as he spent his money on alcohol. Her salary was not anywhere near adequate to support her children alone. As you can see, Sylvia took her motherhood responsibilities very seriously. Sylvia was loath to have to repeat a state of poverty for her children! Even if I wasn't in the picture, she eventually would have found a way to escape her dire circumstances. For, she was sanguine and possessed resolve and determination.

Sylvia's defective marriage was well-known in her family as well as her best female friend (who was her next door neighbor and landlord) and others. So, I'm not exposing a secret. Moreover, the reasons (not the details) for her marital dissolution are public record as is the case in all 50 State and US Territories. There's more to this story that, respectfully, is not being recounted. I am not about the business of impugning this man's reputation. As a mental health professional I felt sorry for him. I never spoke to him. I didn't know him. And, I only saw him once at a distance. Sylvia's ex-husband died on October 16, 1987 of the wicked, vicious disease cancer.

I going to take another break

Naturally, Sylvia being financially challenged, I paid for her divorce which was granted on March 2, 1966.

Before I move on, I want to say a word about domestic abuse. Why? Because it's a more serious problem than professionals and the public are cognizant of. And, hopefully, you'll find something in this book that may help you assist either a victim or an abuser.

There is extensive research and statistics on domestic violence/abuse. The only statistic I care about is the prevalence of this problem. For women the purported rate is about 33%. For men around 20% to 25%. (Yes, some women, in addition to verbally lambasting their significant other, do beat-the-shit out of their man (sometimes woman in a gay relationship). But those percentages are bilge as they are seriously skewed downward and fail to account for the huge number of unreported cases of domestic abuse. In my over 50 years of experience in the mental health field, I believe that the true level of domestic abuse for women victims is at least 50% and maybe even as high as 67%. And, for male victims I'm convinced the rate is at least 40% to as high as 50%. Vexing, isn't it?

Marriage planning

January of 1966 was a time in my life when I was on the fence between being agnostic and maintaining Christianity.

Sometime in the Summer of 1965 I became acquainted with Rev. Lando Eitzen, a Congregational Minister, who was a Chaplin for the State Mental Hospital where Sylvia and I were employed. Lando was quite interested in learning about Rational-Emotive Behavior Therapy. I tutored him. Rev. Eitzen then asked to be a cotherapist with me in providing group therapy to my patients. I consented as we had become good friends and he really liked REBT. Lando proved to be a great therapist; and, even wrote some articles for the REBT Journal.

Sylvia and I discussed and agreed to have Reverend Lando Eitzen marry us.

So it was to be on April 27, 1966 we were married. I was 27 years old. Sylvia was 29 years of age. The Indian couple with whom we went to the St. Louis Muny Opera, Vijay and Esther Dubey, stood up for us at the wedding. No one else was in attendance which was our choice. Our lives didn't really begin until we met each other. (A sentiment echoed by Nancy Reagan about her husband President "Ronnie"). The relationship between Sylvia and I was both fortuitous and serendipitous.

To paraphrase MasterCard's Ad campaign several years ago:

There are some things money can't buy!
Starting a New Life Together – PRICELESS!!!

CHAPTER

SOULMATES

NOT LONG AFTER Sylvia enumerated the sordid details of her miserable marriage, each of us "poured-out our hearts" to each other. Thus, the nascent emergence of Soulmates.

In **Chapter 3, Love at First Sight,** I stated that love-at-first-sight is a strange, undefined and indescribable feeling. The same can be said about Soulmates. More often than not love-at-first sight couples quickly become soulmates. Both are characterized by a strong urge to enter into a relationship with another person.

A soulmate is someone you immediately and strongly connect with in a way never before experienced. Unexplainably drawn to be in a relationship. From there, it evolves into a complex, deep relationship. A bonding that promulgates happiness, comfort, calmness and peace. A harmonious relationship.

Twin Axiomatic Traits of Soulmates

The first axiomatic trait of all soulmates is: ***The inviolable rule of No Secrets! None!! No Sacred Secrets ever!!!*** Thus, the relationship is not encumbered by censorship. This intentionally promotes a strong marriage that is free of emotional foundation cracks. ***The soulmate couple never maintains supersized secrets nor any secrets whatsoever!!!***

The second twin axiomatic trait of all soulmates, is as much a corollary as a twin, is: ***Trust!*** **Sacred trust.** Clearly ***Trust*** is essential to sustain the total absence of secrets. Were talking ***powerful unremitting trust*** of the life-and-death species! Plain and simple ***granite trust!***

What more can be said about Soulmates? A lot! So here are some characteristics or features. A mostly, but not necessarily exhaustive, inventory.

A Soulmate relationship is, by definition, more intense than other relationships. Soulmates are so relationship confident and comfortable that they naturally eyeball each other when conversing. Thus, Soulmates communicate facily.

Soulmates understand each other, are non-judgmental and manifest unqualified acceptance. Briefly, Soulmates have mutual respect and understanding. Therefore, Soulmates have the freedom to say anything and know they are listened to.

Developed over time, Soulmates know what each other is thinking and feeling. This ability leads to the gift of communicating reciprocally nonverbally how they think and feel. For example, when Soulmates smile at each other, they're not only saying "I love you", but also you're my Soulmate!"

Soulmates are content with each other. And, Soulmates are the ultimate upgrade from compatibility. Soulmates have shared values, very similar opinions, beliefs, and attitudes.

It goes without saying, that Soulmates have a highly satisfying sexual liason.

Lest you think a Soulmate relationship is entirely blissful, let me disabuse you of that conception. Since we humans are imperfect, any relationship is definitively deficient. No one's immune to lapses in judgment. Thus, a Soulmate relationship doesn't always run smoothly, nor is it devoid of challenges. That's not a bad thing. It's simply part of individual and couple growth. An evolutionary struggle.

Crises or setbacks exist but are dealt with swiftly. You see, Soulmates are able to compromise effectively and move beyond the issues. Moreover, Soulmates ***recognize and accept*** each other's imperfections. Strife is well- managed.

In some ways, there is a third axiom Soulmates possess. That is: they have long-term relationships (courtship plus marriage) that usually span 50 or more years. Yes, there are some Soulmate relationships that end untimely such as in premature death by illness or accident. Incidentally, a highly gratifying sexual relationship is critical to a long-term Soulmate relationship.

Divorce is non-existent with Soulmate! It just doesn't happen! The divorce rate over the past 50 years is contentious. And, it is still being debated today. I'll forego presenting the pros and cons involved in these studies. Despite valiant efforts by some researchers, I believe their divorce rate conclusions are raffish (disreputable). Therefore, in my humble estimation no one has successfully refuted that the divorce rate remains at 50% to 53%.

The incidence of couple relationships/marriages of 50 or more years is a miniscule 5% to 6%.. Of course it is possible to have a long-lasting and loving (50+ years) relationship without being Soulmates. So if you factor out non-Soulmate alliances and then factor back in early demise of would-have-been long-term bonds, I believe you still have only about 5% of the population that are credibly regarded as Soulmates. Pretty small number don't you think? Is ignorance bliss or hell? In this case, it's probably bliss. Because how can the many satisfying non-Soulmate relationships miss something they never knew existed?

Just for the record. Did you ever stop to think if Hollywood/ Celebrities could be in a Soulmate alliance? Seems like an oxymoron? Hollywood and related personnel are probably the epitome of serial polygamy. There are only 5 famous entertainment couples currently married 25 to 31 years. There may be more I am unaware of.

However, there are two famous Hollywood couples that were incontrovertible Soulmates. The first is the unlikely bond between a Jewish man George Burns and a Catholic woman Gracie Allen. They were married for 38 years (1926 thru 1964). Gracie died on 8-27-64 (the month and day birthday of my wife Sylvia) of a heart attack at age 69. Gracie was born January 20, 1896. George Burns never remarried (an undeniable testimony of a Soulmate). Only, in extremely rare circumstances does a Soulmate remarry. And even then it has to be a second Soulmate! George was 100 years old when he died (03-09-1996).

The second world famous Hollywood Soulmate? You guessed it. President Ronald and Nancy Reagan. President Reagan died at the age of 94 on June 5, 2004. He and Nancy were married for 52 years!. Nancy died on March 6, 2016 at age 93. Again, they had an uncontested Soulmate bond. I'm sure I've overlooked other celebrity Soulmates.

As I write this chapter my mind became peripatetic (wandering and drifting). Finally my thoughts migrated to the mid 1970's. I was teaching a highly specialized Psychology course as an adjunct professor. A student asked, in front of my class, if one or both marital partners kept a diary or journal did that preclude their relationship from being Soulmates? I answered that if the diary/journal were **secret** then the Soulmate relationship was non-existent. Because true, credible Soulmates have no **secrets!** Plus, the dirary/journal keeper, more likely than not, would be the controlling partner in the relationship which also renders the relationship as *unequal.* **True Soulmates have no need for a secret diary/journal. For Soulmates a secret diary/journal is useless and is an *oxymoron.*** Current research reveals that a humongous 83% of females keep a secret diary. Not a good sign.

Finally, Soulmates do not flaunt their intense union! There is no legitimate reason to do so. So, keeping to themselves, as it were, it is quite rare for others including family to be able to recognize that they are Soulmates. Undeniably though, Soulmates deftly identify other Soulmate couples.

So there you have it. As tears of both incredible joy and sadness stream down my face, you know the incomprehensible and excruciating pain brought about by the loss of a ***ONE-OF-A-KIND SOULMATE!!!!!***

Intermission

CHAPTER

ANATOMY OF A HYPERWIFE

SYLVIA HAD A passel of personality assets. I can not begin to expound on the multiplicity of these assets as it would launch me on a tome. Hence, I shall only comment on a few of her exceptional qualities succinctly.

Diagnostic Prowess

There's a back story to Sylvia's mental health diagnostic prowess that dates back to when we first met. You may recall earlier when I stated that we first met at a psychiatric multi disciplinary meeting at the Jacksonville (IL) Mental Hospital. Among other items, those meetings were to obtain patient data to establish a diagnosis. Diagnosing of any type requires knowing the presenting *symptoms.* Without *symptoms*, there can be no diagnosis. All mental health disciplines were required to participate in this process. Psychiatric technicians were in the best position to assess a patient's overt symptoms as they spent the most time with them. Some techs were better at codifying the symptoms. Sylvia was superb. Rarely, if ever, did she not get it right! Sylvia was familiar with the Diagnostic Criteria Manual (DSM) of the American

Psychiatric Association. When Sylvia presented her data, she did so in a diplomatic, low-key, non-threatening manner. I was quite impressed with Sylvia's knowledge of mental health behavior and diagnostic ability. A diagnostic dynamo!

There's a bit more to this story. But, I'm not going to bore you. What I can say though is that Sylvia preferred to remain silent about this skill and many others, for that matter, as I continue to enumerate. It is noteworthy that Sylvia's diagnostic ability was *not a perishable skill. In fact all of Sylvia's assets were non-perishable!!!*

High Octane Intellectual Horsepower

This talent has a more scintillating back story. Recognizing Sylvia's diagnostic facileness, I concluded that she was at least of above average in intelligence. I never really gave her intellectual ability much more thought beyond that.

Sometime toward the end of the Summer of 1966 Sylvia excitedly told me she had just found out about Adult Education High School evening completion courses. I assumed she had a High School diploma. Sylvia explained that she dropped out of High School because she was relentlessly and fiercely harassed, made fun of, ridiculed and hazed because she was poor and had no decent clothes to wear to school. I was stunned by this revelation! At the same time I was so happy for her that she was going finish High School. This was not a GED course. It was a bonafide High School diploma.

When Sylvia came home in the evening from her first day in school she was flabbergasted! She asked enthusiastically: Guess what!? I said, "what"? She said "I got all the same teachers I had before and they all remembered me and really welcomed me!" Each night thereafter Sylvia delightfully wanted to share with me what she learned. These were really enchanting discussions.

Ultimately Sylvia completed her High School diploma course in record time at the top of her class. I can't tell you how happy I was for her!

There's much more to this amazing story. During the time Sylvia was attending the Adult Education High School course we were visited by a door-to-door Encyclopedia Britannica salesman. Throughout his sales pitch Sylvia's eyes were glistening and she was riveted to what he was saying. So I knew I had to buy the Encyclopedias for her and her children (and any children she and I would have). Fortunately, the sales pitch was persuasive and not a hard-sell. To top it off, we got a certificate for a 4 day and 3 night Miami Beach Hotel vacation. [That vacation certificate ended up becoming an annual vacation for us resulting in our eventual relocation to Tampa, Florida in 1979.]

Sylvia's thirst and eagerness to have the Encyclopedias made me ponder more seriously about her intellectual ability.

Before I reveal what I found, I want to say a few words about Intelligence Testing so you know the context and understand.

At this point in my clinical psychology career, I had already logged more than 1,000 Intelligent Quotient((IQ) evaluations. The onset of IQ testing and scores was in the early 1900's. There are several different IQ tests available for professional use. The two most popular are the Stanford-Binet and the Wechsler Adult Intelligence Scale (WAIS) and it's sister the Wechsler Intelligence Scale for Children (WISC). The Stanford-Binet came out in 1916 with the most recent 5th edition in 2003. The WAIS/WISC were released in 1939 and the WAIS IV revised edition was published in 2008. I discontinued psychological testing in the year 2000, having performed several hundred. I had also tested the IQ's for those wanting to be certified to join the high IQ society MENSA.

All IQ tests have a numerical range which is associated with a descriptive category. For example, 90 to 109 on a given test would be considered Average. But that same numerical range might be called something else on another test. Some IQ tests go as high as 199. Whereas the highest range for most other IQ tests is 130 to 150. The actual number is not important. The descriptive classification is the significant factor. All of the IQ tests do have consistency in their descriptive classifications. Ignoring Below Average and lower descriptions, the IQ descriptions are: Average, Above Average, Superior, and Very Superior.

The top category, Very Superior has and is variously referred to as genius, gifted, profoundly gifted and exceptionally gifted. Persons with this IQ are in the upper 2%to 3% of the population. They are doctors of all types, scientists, dentists and many other professions. Even a very small number people without any college or advanced degrees can have a top IQ. These lesser educated people who are intellectually Very Superior almost always have faced extenuating circumstances, or lack of opportunity or just never had the wherewithal to obtain more education.

There are both formal and informal IQ measurements that can be done. These measurements are both valid and highly reliable. Therefore, a seasoned veteran IQ tester can, if necessary, determine an IQ surreptitiously. Ethical considerations do not allow me to elaborate further.

Now for my brain shock. The results of Sylvia's I.Q. assessment placed her in the top, Very Superior, category. Being the unique personality she was, retreating from any semblance of trying to impress anyone, Sylvia wanted to remain quiet and private about her high octane intellectual horsepower!

I don't want to convey the impression that those who have Very Superior Intellects are omniscient or all-knowing. Clearly, no one is! There are esoteric facts that escape even the most intelligent of those among us. Try this on for size. Ask any highly intelligent person you know (except a mathematician or physicist), such as your health doctor or pharmacist, dentist, veterinarian or even a master chef, to define the ***fibonacci sequence.*** I guarantee you they won't know the answer, just as you don't right now. So, look it up on the internet. You'll be thankful.

The common denominator of those imbued with a Very Superior intellect is: Highly Superior Memory. This is not to be confused with ***Hyperthymesia*** or ***Hyperthymesia Syndrome*** which is also known as ***HSAM. HSAM*** is short for ***Highly Superior Autobiographical Memory.*** This is a condition wherein the person has an extremely detailed autobiographical memory. These people recall pretty much perfectly an inordinate number of their experiences including exact days and dates as well as places. This ability is probably more of a burden than a blessing. Their memories are encoded involuntarily and retrieved automatically. It is a purely subconscious process (since only the subconscious can access the memory bank). Otherwise, those with ***HSAM*** have average memories in all other areas.

You may be puzzled as to why I'm providing you with this data. The answer is: it is not uncommon for many grieving persons – having lost a loved one(s) – to experience numerous flashbacks (fueled by regret, remorse, guilt etc.) about their relationship with their loved one(s) the *mimics* **Highly Superior Autobiographical Memory**. But that type of experience does not qualify as HSAM.

While I'm speaking of Very Superior Memory, I might as well make it complete.

There are three (3) other noteworthy High Memory platforms.

The first is called ***Idiot Savant*** or sometimes just ***Savant.*** Savant is French (which was my foreign language college course) for "learned". So the complete translation is "learned idiot". It is a prodigy person who displays brilliance in one area, skill, or talent particularly involving outstanding memory such as in music/musical instrument performing or numbers and so on. Otherwise, these persons are mentally handicapped with way below average overall I.Q.'s, many having *autism spectrum disorder,* in all other areas on intellectual functioning.

These last two (2) memory platforms only occur with those who have Very Superior Memory Endowment. And, they are self-explanatory. *Total Recall* and *Photographic Memory.* Only a very tiny percentage within the upper 3% of the population (Very Superior I.Q.) have the fantastic ability of Total Recall or Photographic Memory.

Prescient

Take your pick: foreknowledge of events, foresight, to know beforehand. The ability to know what will or might transpire in the future; prophetic, predictive, visionary, perceptive. My choice? ***INTUITIVE*** along with other adjectives.

Sylvia had the dominant ability to "read" a stranger with supersonic speed. The word ***nanosecond*** comes to mind. If you think I'm exaggerating, try this research on for size.

A Princeton University psychologist found (2006) that "***Snap Judgments decide a face's character...First Impressions: Making Up Your Mind After a 100 millisecond Exposure to a Face.***"

This groundbreaking psychological research noted that in spite of our being cautioned not to judge a book by its cover, "our brains decide whether a person ***is attractive and trustworthy within a tenth of a second".*** The psychologist author, Alex Todorov, observed that "...people respond ***intuitively*** to faces so rapidly that our reasoning minds may not have time to influence the reaction – and that our ***intuitions*** about attraction and trust are among those we form the fastest." Todorov went on to say "We decide very quickly whether a person possesses many of the traits we feel important, such as likeability and competence, even though we have not exchanged a single word with them. It appears as if we are hard-wired to draw these inferences in a fast, unreflective way." Thus, without sufficient time for rational thought, we make snap judgments on character. This research involved timed experiments of 100 milliseconds and 500 milliseconds or a full second.

Related to snap judgments is a 2015 study conducted by Bangor University linguistics professor Vyv Evans. Evans said: "There are estimates that as much as 70% of the meaning we derive from a face-to-face encounter with someone comes from non-verbal cues: facial expressions, intonation, body language, pitch. Which means words account for only around 30% of what we say."

So virtually all of us make snap judgments based on non-verbal cues. With the passing of time, though, we are able to make corrections in our judgments when necessary.

What separates Sylvia from virtually everyone else is her judgmental speed and accuracy rarely requiring subsequent tweaking in judgment. A nanosecond is billionth of a second which is faster than 100 or 500 milliseconds. I stand by my assertion that Sylvia's ***intuitive*** talent only took a nanosecond. Her intuitive ability ranked way beyond what most of us have. Intuition is both genetic and developed. The brain part (amygdala) that responds to fear is considered to be involved in judgments of trustworthiness. Since Sylvia was raised in abject poverty and ostracized in both Grade and High School, you can see where to survive she became hypervigilant and fearful. Beyond what was innate, it was those early experiences that contributed to the development of her profound ***intuition! A level of intuition I have never before seen in anyone!!!*** Though I'm reasonably confident there are a rare few who have a similar talent.

To put this in perspective, I throw this in to show you Sylvia's specialness. The Israeli Airport Security Forces are the most sophisticated, advanced bad-guy detectors in the world. They have an almost 100% record of success. A few years back the United States Government enlisted the Israelis to train TSA (Transportation Security Administration) personnel in their screening methodology. My point is that Sylvia's ***Intuitive*** talent even without Israeli training would have rivaled their best. Can you imagine what she would have been with some training? One helluva force to be reckoned with!!! She was just that special! Circumstances permitting, her goal was to become a law enforcement detective. Wouldn't you agree she would have been a cut-above, excellent detective? She possessed the unique ability to surreptitiously disarm others. (To be sure, Sylvia also aspired to be an actress).

Once again, Sylvia wanted to remain private, for the most part, about this high-powered skill.

Gregarious

Sylvia was a very charming, humble and sociable woman. She could light up a room full of people just by her presence. She had a beautiful, infectious smile. Dr. Albert Ellis remarked, when he met her (1965) that Sylvia's smile was captivating.

Sylvia had a masterful ability to make anyone feel totally comfortable and trusting when you first met her. She readily engendered trust. Once she engaged you, you were her friend for life. Upon subsequent encounters, Sylvia would want to know how you were doing along with all the other family members you told her about.

So picture this. You're walking along and Sylvia encounters you and she says: "Oh, I really like your shoes". Time permitting, off to the races you go conversationally. Sylvia could always find something complimentary to say to a stranger. A stranger would always recognize Sylvia's unconditional acceptance. And, as a result, the stranger felt Sylvia regarded them as important. The upshot, virtually always, was that the stranger(s) poured out their life history. So, if Sylvia struck up a conversation with a stranger in the airport while I was in the bathroom by the time I got back she already had their life history.

Sylvia was an outgoing, kind hearted woman. She was always sincerely interested in your life and that of your family. Thus you felt good in meeting with her.

Sylvia appreciated everyone regardless of their position in life. Too she was not intimated by anyone. She easily recognized wealthy and "old money" people and facilely engaged in discourse with them. I was awestruck at the ease with which total strangers revealed themselves to Sylvia.

She was a model of politeness, respect, compassion and caring. Finally, Sylvia had a deep, hearty, infectious laugh displaying much joy.

A Superior Mother

Sylvia desperately wanted a better life for her children. To her, that meant that she had to be the best mother possible.

At the very beginning of our marriage, she was reluctant to have me participate in the discipline process. No conflict emerged. Why? Because Sylvia was able to appeal, skillfully, to higher purposes. And, because I recognized that it was an adjustment transition that would eventually be resolved.

I failed to note earlier, that after only 11 moths of marriage, Sylvia became pregnant with her 5th child. On Pearl Harbor Day, December 7, 1967 our daughter was born. Were the child to have been a boy we would have named it John, II. A girl we decided to name Sylvia, II. What better way to honor my wife than to have our daughter named after her? That was before the Women's Liberation Movement started, which was in 1969.

Subtly, tactfully and idiosyncratically Sylvia conveyed the message to her children: Be respectful, courteous and learn. You could say it was an in-your-face admonition with unconditional love. She had a knack for communicating a point firmly without recrimination.

Sometime around 3 or so years after we were married, I asked Sylvia if she wanted me to help out financially if any of her children wanted to attend college. Sylvia said: "No, John, that's not your responsibility. That would be their father's responsibility. You've done more than I ever dreamed would happen. You provided homes and furniture for 4 of my children. You feed them. You clothed them. You provided gifts for them. You helped me raise them. You did far more than their father ever did. He just abandoned them. I hate to think of what my life as a mother would have been like without you."

So that's just how Sylvia's thought process worked. She never demanded anything. She was always appreciative of what we had as a couple raising children.

Parenthetically, I was raised with Italian cultural familial values (which are also imbued in other cultures). Sadly, this value system is wrong-headedly regarded by outsiders as controlling. Nothing could be further from the truth. This value system posits that the man has the responsibility to provide for his family. Anything less is grounds for being chastised, severe criticism, retribution or, at the very least, other negative consequences. Control is not the issue. ***Fear is the issue!!!*** [That doesn't mean some Italian men aren't controlling.]

There are nuances of this value system I'll forego detailing. The point is that this Italian family value system does have limitations. It took me some time to come to grips with that stark reality. The problem with this lone ranger status is the husband/father is the hierarchial head which relegates the other family members to being dependent. A growth impediment. And, thus marginalized. The other family members' independence is hi-jacked. So, the lesson I had to learn was how ***not*** to take charge. Simply be ***responsible!*** I largely, but not 100%, conquered this issue.

Sylvia had a very responsible fourfold parental philosophy. First a parent desirably demonstrates unconditional love. Second, do everything possible to ensure that the chil(ren) learns and is, thus, educated. Third, teach the child(ren) to be respectful, courteous, kind and compassionate toward others. And, fourth, a parent has the duty to be supportive but not in a counseling context. She adamantly believed that parents should not be a therapist or counselor to their child(ren). That job is for someone else, preferably a professional. There is a fine line to be walked between being supportive and a therapist. Sylvia walked that line stealthily, almost always.

Sylvia knew each of her children were different and was adroit in handling them. Each child required a different skill set for her to utilize. I simply marveled and was awestruck with how she dealt with each of her children. It was a thing of beauty to observe. Wow!!! The combination of Sylvia's very superior intellectual endowment and her off-the-charts intuitiveness allowed her to know each of her children exceptionally well. Sylvia knew every asset and weakness of each of her children. I can add unqualifiedly that Sylvia knew her children better than they knew themselves. Judiciously, she refused to interfere in their lives with her knowledge. That, my friends, is a monumental feat and mute testimony to an accomplished mother.

Homemaker

Sylvia was thrust into a homemaker role very early in her life. She was 17 years old and her first child was only a few months old. From that time until we got married, she acquired 12 years of experience.

I was quite pleased with how Sylvia discharged her homemaking duties. I hasten to add that we both shared in all household chores. She was fastidious about maintaining a clean and orderly home. No easy task with 4 children initially followed by a fifth a few months later. She paid attention to detail not only in the household but also in her family and her overall life. Which means she was very observant. Noteworthy and remotely related to homemaking (attention and observation) is Sylvia's proficiency to be in a crowded venue (e.g. restaurant) and focus on up to 4 different conversations simultaneously and report what was going down. Astounding, don't you agree?

Sylvia was a master at multi-tasking; and somewhat ambidextrous though predominantly right-handed.

She was a truly good and creative home cook almost entirely self-taught.

So the bottom line is that Sylvia was quite proficient at all Homemaking obligations.

Well-Rounded

I was going to alliterate all of the entertainment/educational genre TV programs and specific shows related thereto. I decided that would be a bit much. So, I'm just going portray the general categories and you can aptly fill-in-the-blanks.

The fine arts. You already know that Sylvia loved Municipal Operas. So, it's no wonder that she equally loved Broadway plays. Actually she embraced virtually of the fine arts activities, especially paintings. She, herself, had minimal training in acrylic et al painting either in person or on educational TV. But she pounded-out some pretty potent beautiful paintings. Sadly, she wasn't able to find enough available leisure time to do more painting. She particularly liked Salvatore Dali's work.

Sylvia enjoyed all types of educational TV programs like History, National Geographic, The Learning Channel.

Too, Sylvia was fascinated with animal programs such as Cats, Westminister Dog Show, Pit Bull shows etc.

Sylvia liked all kinds of Sports programs: College and Pro football, Figure Skating, Gymnastics, Winter and Summer Olympics, Golf, Tennis, Cheerleader competition, Water Sports etc. She thoroughly enjoyed water-skiing and pleasure boating.

Here's an incomplete list of the types of TV and life programs she cherished: Cooking shows (both educational and competitive, kids and adults); Reality TV; Soaps; Competition shows like Survivor/The Amazing Race; Circus shows like Cirque de soleil; Comedy; Sitcoms like Golden Girls, Friends etc.; Musical and Talent shows such as American Idol, America's Got Talent and Dancing with the Stars. She loved to dance and was accomplished at it.

Her favorite books and TV programs involved law enforcement/ detective issues. You may recall that I noted above that she aspired to be a detective. Too, Sylvia was a avid reader. Traveling was always a wonderful experience for Sylvia. She was especially fond of our annual Las Vegas trips.

Sylvia enjoyed playing board games as well as card games like pinochle, poker, and gin rummy.

I'm going to stop here and forego any further illustrations. How more well-rounded can anyone be?

Phoenix

Sylvia rocketed full-throttle from the ashes of oppressive poverty straight through gentrification to the pinnacle upper class in terms of tastes and values, not financial status. Her taste in material goods was florid. For, she eschewed flamboyance and extravagance. I'm thankful that I was always able to give here what few material possessions she asked for. In rare instances, it sometimes took me a couple of years "to come around."

For me (since I'm the only one that counts) Sylvia was stunningly beautiful and sexy. If ever there was a classy elegant woman, Sylvia was the personification. Think Audrey or Katherine Hepburn even Sophia Loren or Grace Kelly. Maybe even Sally field.

Don't like any of these picks/comparisons (as a family member)? Who would your nominees be? Then, maybe, no one fits-the-bill!. Because Sylvia was **truly one-of-a-kind!**

Difficulties

All of us have flaws, deficiencies, faults and failings. Sylvia was no different. For the most part these all-too-human frailties for Sylvia were not that significant or handicapping. Thus, there is no reason to recite them. There were only a paucity anyway.

There were two issues that gripped her which she had to grapple with periodically. Back in the day, the psychiatric/psychological nomenclature would have been different. Nowadays it is termed ***Post-Traumatic Stress Syndrome or PTSD.***

Post-Traumatic Stress Disorder occurs following a traumatic, threatening ordeal involving actual or physical harm to you, a loved one or even a stranger. Usual symptoms can include flashbacks of the event, recurring memories and nightmares that often elicit shame and guilt, and a multitude of other powerful negative feelings. These symptoms can wax and wane; come and go; travel underground mentally for long periods only later to erupt like a volcano. This disorder is emotionally and mentally persistent consequent to severe psychological shock.

PTSD # 1. As a young girl, Sylvia was a victim of licentious (morally unrestrained sexual) behavior. Commonly referred to as sex abuse or sexual molestation. Sylvia unveiled, actually bared-her-soul, to me this traumatic experience shortly after our first date. The fact that she was forthcoming about this sex abuse was good. The fact that I was ultimately able to help her overcome this within our intimate relationship was nice. The fact that she **trusted me to assist her in this matter was epic and monumental!!!**

This traumatic sexual experience bothered Sylvia throughout her entire life. Not on a daily basis. Whenever she became aware of bad sexual conduct such as in a conversation with someone, on the TV News or in a TV show or movie, she had to relive these intense negative emotions. Even worse and extremely challenging was for her to be in the presence of someone she knew or suspected of having manifested undesirable sexual behavior. Sometimes these powerful negative feelings just emerged from seemingly nowhere. Virtually no one was cognizant of her feelings except for me as she was an expert at masking her emotions in this context.

PTSD # 2. You already know the extent to which Sylvia was exposed to alcoholism. First her father. Then her first husband.

The statistics about alcoholism haven't changed appreciably since when I first began treating this group over 50 years ago. Sylvia knew that the research reported cause of alcoholism is 50% environmental and 50% genetic. She also knew that the children of alcoholics were 8 times more likely to become alcoholic than the general population. And, that the children of alcoholics had anywhere from a 25% to 50% chance of becoming addicted to alcohol.

So Sylvia's Post-Traumatic Stress Disorder in this context was a combination of both family alcoholism and the associated domestic violence.

Inasmuch as possible she preferred to not be around others if she thought they might over drink as that aroused bad memories. Being prescient she was able to detect the smallest behavioral changes in someone's alcohol-related behavior. In order to minimize her tyrannical PTSD emotional responses, she only wanted to remain at any event for at most a couple of hours. Important is Sylvia's belief that she didn't think it was right or appropriate for her to make known to anyone how she felt. Her attitude was that others had the right to pursue whatever path they chose.

Sylvia wasn't a teetotaler. She did have an occasional beer or glass of wine. The last seven years of her life witnessed an almost complete abstinence from alcohol as a result of a stroke in January of 2008.

Since I respected Sylvia's desire to remain private about this matter, it was only known to us. For Sylvia, it was important to remain low key under-the-radar in connection with some of her abilities as well as some of her values.

Can you imagine the detrimental, bring-to-your-knees, cry-uncle emotional pain Sylvia would have experienced if both these PTSD's converged simultaneously? Truly dismayed, don't you reckon? Daunting, crushing and grisly results! Did it happen? Yes! More than once but infrequently.

Some Final Thoughts

Sylvia was a strong woman. A woman of character. She was supremely kind; and "kind" was one of her favorite words. Only she and I knew what "kind" meant to her. For Sylvia to remark that someone was kind to her, she meant that person truly cared about her. That that person was deeply concerned about her. That she was important to him/her. And, that they treated her gently.

Over time special /holiday gift-giving became progressively and incrementally less important for both of us. Something not uncommon for soulmates. We developed more flexibility to the point where either no or minimal gift-giving on a special day or holiday. This was supplanted by larger gift purchases at different times throughout the year. For instance, I might give Sylvia a cash gift before Christmas to spend as she wished during a vacation in Las Vegas. Our frequent Las Vegas vacations took place on or after Thanksgiving but before Christmas. This flexibility proved more to our mutual satisfaction.

Christmas, for Sylvia, was very important because it was non-existent for her as a child stemming from crippling oppressive poverty. I never lost sight of that. Although, I did "tease" her about it. I made damn sure I always took good care of her for Christmas. This gift-giving transshaping was a quiet agreement just between us.

From the onset of our marriage up until about 3 weeks before she passed away (a span of nearly 50 years) Sylvia consistently announced to any stranger we met: "He married me with 4 kids I don't think I could have done it." Early on I quickly realized what she was saying to me as a soulmate: "John, I love you for you and what you have done for me and my children. I'm grateful for our relationship and mutual devotion." I could see it in her riveting eyes. It was totally non-verbal, which is exactly how soulmates communicate. Each of us knew how to "read between the lines." I have to stop for a moment now.

So that's my psychological autopsy of my brilliant beloved wife **Sylvia Loreen Gullo.** We had an intransigent mutual commitment. I'm not going to say maybe I could have done better. That would be dishonest! I've done the very best I know how. And I tell you I don't know how I could have done any better. I gave it my all. I gave every bit I could give. Nothing less. I passionately poured all of my heart and soul into this treatise!

• •

This begs the question:

Does a Child(ren) Really Know Their Parent(s)?

Before this is answered, I'd like you to ponder and answer these questions. Do you know much about your mother's or father's (includes a step- or foster parent) life before any child(ren) was/were born? Do you know any uncomfortable "secrets" about your parent(s)? Do you know all about your parents' sex life? Do you know the ***nuances*** (grey areas) of your parents' values/philosophies? Do you really think your parents want you (or anyone for that matter excepting a spouse) to know them 100%? What "secrets" and/or undesirable regretful behaviors are you hiding? What are you holding back on? If you have children, what are you keeping from them? For that matter, what are you hiding from your own family members?

I could go on, but I think you get the idea/picture and know the answer as well.

In late August of 1968, at an American Psychological Convention in San Francisco, CA I participated with Dr. Albert Ellis and three (3) other Rational-Emotive Behavior Therapy (REBT) clinical psychologists in an all-day workshop/seminar on REBT. Dr. Ellis was giving a live therapy demonstration with a psychologist attendee. During this live exhibition therapy session Dr. Ellis remarked that he began his career as a Marriage and Family Psychotherapist. Dr. Ellis went on to explain, unequivocally, that a child or children, as the case may be, "never really know there parents that well."

As unsettling as it may be, that's an undeniable reality!

I, retrospectively, knew very little about my parents. Over the years, I was very surprised to discover (after my parents passed) "things" about them that I never knew.

Children's views of their parents tend to be shaped quixotically. That is, framed unrealistically, idealistically or impractically, not to mention filled with ignorance. Over 50 years in the mental health business has taught me that rare indeed are children who know much about their parents let alone any siblings and even other family members.

I have gleefully exposed all that is allowable about whom the **real Sylvia really was. My unyielding, fierce loyalty precludes any further disclosure!**

It would be nice if you had the opportunity to really know Sylvia as I do.

It has been a downright privilege and honor to dutifully reveal my wife's truly amazing life!!!

As Sylvia's children, you should be proud and honored to have had such an incredible mother!!! And, you should have an extreme sense of satisfaction about you mother!!! Not many children have the good fortune to have an unconditionally loving mother like Sylvia!!!!!!!!!!!!!!!!!!!!!!!!!!!!!!.

CHAPTER

CAREGIVING

ON SEPTEMBER 28, 2015 (5 months and 2 weeks after my wife's untimely passing) I sent an E-mail to my 2 brothers and sister. The E-mail was entitled: "John's becoming a widower." It was my attempt to help them understand mine and Sylvia's 51 year relationship. That E-mail only stated with much brevity what I detailed earlier in the Chapters on **Love At First Sight and Soulmates.**

By sharing the relevant parts of this E-mail (without duplicating what I said in earlier Chapters herein), I think can spotlight the issue of caregiving. Any ***bracketed*** information interspersed in the context is for explanation or expansion purposes.

"I've been meaning to send this E-mail for some time. Finally, I'm doing it even though I've known it was going to be gut-wrenching to do it. I think I've been remiss in trying to **really** explain the overwhelming...experience I've undergone losing my wife Sylvia. I'm going to do the best I can, though weeping...in the process, to try to explain this monumentally unfortunate experience...[I went on to succinctly explain **Love At First Sight and Soulmates]**

In January of 2008 Sylvia had a Stroke that resulted in her having **expressive aphasia – great difficulty in her expressing herself verbally.** [With expressive aphasia the person knows what they want to say but just can't say the word, so they try to find another word(s). Sylvia was born with a mild degree of expressive aphasia. The Stroke worsened her expressive aphasia.] But because she and I knew each other 'like a book', I knew what she was trying to say. Our daughter Sylvia,II was second in knowing what her mother was trying to communicate because daughter Sylvia [who has always lived with us] was the...person who **nursed** her mother with constant mental exercises to 'repair' the brain damage caused by the Stroke. I did what I could as I was caught between trying to continue to work and setting aside time to help Sylvia 'recover'. I did fly her to Missouri [from Tampa, FL] about 3 weeks after her Stroke to get the **Oxygen bath** treatment [pump a high level of oxygen to the brain to accelerate healing],which did help her quite a bit. I wish [retrospectively] I'd had done more because our daughter, Sylvia, II,...[became severely stressed-out] from her intense efforts rehabilitating her mother. Sylvia, II never complained about her efforts and often didn't let me [or anyone else] know how she was cognitively helping her mother.

[My caregiving role began in January of 2008.]

The brain cancer surgery [large diffuse B cell lymphoma on opposite side of her head from where the Stroke occurred] in March of 2014 rendered my wife, Sylvia, with more **expressive aphasia** plus **receptive aphasia** (the inability to understand).That increased my stress enormously...In spite of Sylvia's aphasias, I almost always knew what she was thinking and feeling. Usually all I had to do was look into her eyes. And, I believe, she knew I knew.

From March of 2014 until...Sylvia passed away April 7th [2015], I knew I was going to be her 24/7 caregiver with daughter Sylvia II helping. [I had already closed my Office in 2013] I knew I had to put my wife on a strict [high protein] diet [older people require from 50 to 100 grams of protein daily depending upon their body weight] to maintain her immune system to function as close as possible at 100% to fight any cancer reoccurrence. I compulsively cared for my wife in an attempt to have her 'recover'. [I meticulously examined the nutritional contents of all the food I fed her. This included grams of protein, calories etc. And, I kept a daily log of this data.] I had to get her up in the morning and put her to bed at regular times. I had to wipe her butt after a bowel movement and change her clothes multiple times daily. I had to try to figure out what foods she would like to eat [menu planning] that would be immune system promoting as her taste buds changed from time to time [fickleness] from the brain cancer. Sometimes I even had to 'force' her to eat in order to be properly nourished. **That was gut-wrenching to do!** I had to dress and undress and bath her daily. I had to help her walk. I could go on and on but I think you get the point. [Sylvia's three other children who live in the Tampa Bay area did sometimes provide assistance when they came to visit.]

[Additionally, I experienced unrelenting self-imposed pressure to maintain Sylvia's hygiene meticulously to prevent a UTI (urinary tract infection, which is common in older women and she had several). This relentless pressure also included managing multiple medications and monitoring her diabetic blood sugar. I was engulfed with a pervasive and massive sense of hopelessness in trying to keep her alive. I never realized the debilitating emotional impact of having someone's life in you hands. My self-created stress level was so high I lost 30 lbs in a short period of time without realizing it.]

No one knows (except largely daughter Sylvia II) **what I tried to do to save my Wife's life. No one knows the amount of time and money I spent to 'cure' my wife's medical condition with specialized medicine!** [I was able to obtain a brand new cancer drug just coming on the market that ostensibly could cure the cancer with one dose. She had two doses! New cancer drugs are costly! I spared no time or money! I didn't care what it cost because Sylvia's life was at stake]. Except I do somewhat regret not taking Sylvia to Mexico for treatment, even though the travel would have been enormously difficult! **In the end, I failed miserably to keep my wife alive!!! That is really depressing!!! My only consolation is maybe God was ready to take her and I couldn't have done better!**

I've done the best I can to try and give you a better understanding of my...experience in losing my wife Sylvia. Even though I don't believe anyone can really know what I've been through unless they've undergone pretty much the same or very similar experience. And, that's not casting blame or 'putting down' anyone.

That's just what it is!"

I want to clarify my caregiving role. As my wife Sylvia's caregiver I had to constantly battle my intense fear, anxiety and depression of losing her. I had unremitting relentless pressure to keep her properly nourished and try to "cure" her disease. Striving to maintain freedom from self-imposed emotional turmoil and save and care for my wife was a daunting task!!! I didn't do a very good job in preventing myself from being stressed out.

(It is worth noting that virtually all caregivers are women. Either a daughter or some other female family member. A male caregiver is extremely rare. In the absence of a female (or rare male) family caregiver, the patient's destiny ends very badly in some type of medical facility. So, if you ever encounter this situation do your very best to not let your loved one be placed outside their home! Think about it. If it were you in that circumstance would you want to die alone with no loved ones caring for you!? Damn it, what about some unconditional compassion!?)

Others, including mental health professionals, can assert that they understand what it's like to be a caregiver. I take serious issue with that claim! Not in an attempt to gain sympathy or appear melodramatic. I believe others are sincere in their belief that they understand a caregivers role, but they are truly ignorant and are looking through cataract lenses.

Here are two examples to solidify my contention that only a caregiver knows what it takes to be a caregiver.

The first is a quote from Dr. Paul Kalanithi, M.D. in his posthumously published 2016 book ***When Breath Becomes Air.*** Dr. Kalanithi said: "As a doctor you have a sense of what it's like to be sick, but until you've gone through it yourself, you really don't know. It's like falling in love or having a kid."

The second example I present in the form of a question. Do you, or anyone, know exactly what it's like to have a **"near death experience?"**

Only, another person who has undergone a "near death experience" can know what it's like. Or how about those persons who been "raised-from-the dead" two or three hours after having been definitively declared medically dead. Only those people know what that experience is like.

As a bonus, and at no extra charge, I offer you another perspicacious quote. One of the world's greatest minds, Albert Einstein, had this to say: *"The only source of knowledge is **experience!"***

Don't you think the forgoing examples are incontrovertible and unassailable!? With that I rest my case!!!

I truly hope none of you ever have to undergo the brutal experience of being a 24/7 caregiver!!!

CHAPTER

MOVING ON: GRIEF HEALING

**"Men feel disturbed not by things,
but by the views which they take of them."**
1st Century AD, **Epictetus** in the ***Enchiridion***

THAT FAMOUS ROMAN stoic philosopher's statement encapsulates the cause and cure of mankind's psychological ailments! Many centuries later William Shakespeare rephrased this thought in *Hamlet:* "There (exists) nothing either good or bad but thinking makes it so.

We humans have the unique ability to think both **rationally** and **irrationally.** The most powerful engine of change is **thought – rational, reality-based thought.** Wouldn't it be so wonderful if we had a self-cleaning brain?

This book is not intended to be a comprehensive discourse on Rational-Emotive Behavior Therapy. I am only going to discuss two issues as they relate to grief: Self-confidence and Depression.

Self-Confidence

Much of our emotional responses, globally, hinges on our ability to be and feel self-accepting.

As a human being, you are an ongoing process, constantly changing from birth until death, consisting of a set of likes and dislikes. Since we are continually changing, even our likes and dislikes are changing. Today we may like cheese sandwiches, and tomorrow we may hate them. From the time we are born, our bodies are steadily being altered and aging. As the years go by, we gradually look a bit different. Our attitudes, values and beliefs are continually changing as well – even though we may maintain some attitudes for a lifetime. As a child, you thought it was important to play with toys and dolls. Now, as an adult, you wouldn't think of playing with those same dolls and toys. As a child you probably sucked on lollypops, but now not so much. Therefore, since you are in a constant state of flux, there is no permanent, unchanging you. In other words, you are only a changing you. You simply flow through life growing and maturing. Unfortunately along this evolving road of life we do erect dams that hinder and block us from achieving our full potential.

The principal reason for people have low self-confidence is having learned a false belief about human worth and confusing **work confidence** with **self-confidence. Work confidence** means you know you **can** do something that you would like to do, because you have already proven, by your past behavior, that you have done it or something like it. A person who never tried to walk would hardly acquire confidence in their ability to walk – or swim, or ride a bicycle, or do any other kind of muscular activity

Our society wrongfully teaches us that we **must** and **need** to succeed at tasks and projects. Thus, most of our "pride" or "self-confidence" consists of **false pride** and **false confidence derived from a dire need to succeed.**

You get **work confidence** or **love confidence** by proving, in action, that you can achieve at work or win at love. You can enjoyably have these feelings. Knowing that you can do well at achievement or love, you feel more motivated to strive for future rewards in these areas.

True self-confidence or self-acceptance means that you accept yourself as a valuable person simply because you are alive and can choose to do things that are enjoyable to you.

More importantly, being **truly** self-confident means knowing and understanding that there **is no such thing as human worth.** Let me explain. In order for a human being to be *worthwhile*, you would have to be able to prove that from birth until now all you ever did were good, valuable and worthwhile behaviors. That means you would have to have been perfect! Of course, that is virtually impossible to prove. Moreover, even if you could find such a perfect person, you'd have to be able to prove that from now until their expiration they would continue to act perfectly. You certainly couldn't prove that. So the worthwhile person simply doesn't exist.

By the same reasoning, in order to be a worthless person, you would have to be able to show that from birth until now all you ever did were bad, immoral, worthless behaviors. You would have to be a perfect screwer-upper. Similarly, such an individual is non-existent. Once again, even if this person did exist, you would still have to validate that for the rest of time, they would continue to act in always a despicable manner. This can not be validated.

So, you see, there is no such thing as a **worthwhile** or **worthless** person.

Underlying this common (and ubiquitous) belief in human worth is the idea that *you are your behavior* or that *your behavior is you.* **Your behavior is not you.** And, your behavior can never be you! You, as a whole person, can not logically be given a rating as you might get on a report card. Your behavior is not **you – it is only a part of you.** You, as a whole person, consist of **all** of your behaviors – both the goods and the bads. Hence, you are a person who does good things and bad things. But you can never be a good person or a bad person. You are not a worm for acting wormily. You are not a shit for acting shitily. You are a person who does bad things or makes mistakes, but you can never be a bad person. You are a person who acts asininely from time to time. But you can never be an ass or jackass.

So, you see you don't ever have to rate, value, measure or evaluate "yourself". By ceding such evaluating, self-rating or ego measurement, you practically eviscerate all of your most serious emotional issues or problems in living.

It's okay to rate your **behavior** as good or bad, right or wrong, moral or immoral. But, **you** never have to give **yourself** as a whole person any kind of rating.

True self-confidence means never rating yourself as good or bad! By not rating yourself as a good or bad person enables you to pursue anything you want to do. You do it because you want to do it. You want to learn it. You want to experience it. You don't learn, experience or accomplish anything until you go through the effort of doing and performing. Since you want to be self-confident, you simply do what you want to do and stubbornly refuse to give yourself a rating!

Understand that no one can ever logically judge anyone else. Put differently, no one is qualified to rate you as worthwhile or worthless. Refuse to judge yourself by one piece of behavior!

The idea of something being good or bad is completely relative. It is not etched in stone or absolute. What may be good behavior today may be bad behavior in the future. What was once bad behavior may now be good behavior. So stubbornly refrain from judging yourself at all! You and your actions are not the same because your actions are only a part of you. Thereby you eliminate **feeling** inferior by regarding only your behavior as inferior. Inferior behaviors, **yes**. Inferior people, **no**.

Just as it is illogical to judge yourself or others, similarly it is illogical to condemn yourself or others! We are all simply imperfect, fallible, mistake-making beings. It is very important that you reverse your self-image and free yourself from the crippling distortion of being worthwhile or worthless! Unconditional self-acceptance **(USA)** is the goal. That is also known as **Self-Compassion.**

Depression

It's my job, now, to demonstrate how easy it is to for you to be a self-feeder and overcome your depressive habits.

Dr. Paul Hauck, Ph.D. is a long time friend and Rational-Emotive Behavior Therapy(REBT) clinical psychologist colleague of mine. Dr. Hauck wrote several books on REBT and contributed a chapter (as did I, noted earlier) for Dr. Albert Ellis' book *Growth Through Reason* (1971). Dr. Hauck retired from the private practice of clinical psychology at the age of 82 on July 3, 2007. His practice was in Rock Island, Illinois. So, at this point in time, he would be 91 years old. I want to recognize, acknowledge and represent Dr. Hauck's significant contribution to Rational-Emotive Behavior Therapy. In 1973, Dr. Hauck published the book *Overcoming Depression* wherein he described the Ellis/REBT concept/view of depression in detail. Thus, I have summarized/paraphrased Dr. Hauck's work in less than 500 words. Material that is bracketed, [], represents insertions of my own independent statements, comments and observations. My summary of Dr. Hauck's book begins now.

There are three (3) causes of depression: *Self-blame, self-pity and other-pity.* [Normally all three are involved with ***grief!*** The result is **intellectual bankruptcy.]**

Self-Blame is a product of steadily, constantly putting yourself down, despising yourself and believing you are the worst person alive. [Stated pejoratively: believing you are a total shit.] It really doesn't make any difference what you blame yourself for as long as you give yourself a good poisonous tongue-lashing. Just castigate yourself profoundly and bam you are depressed! Condemn yourself severely, intensely you may even entertain suicide.

Self-Pity, the second cause of depression, is born when you feel sorry for yourself. Cry over not being treated fairly and you quickly become depressed. Try to garner others sympathy by looking down-in-the-dumps and you just boarded a train to depression. Discovering how unfair the world is and wrongly believing it owes you a living, presto you are maudlin.

It may be shocking for you to realize that it is utterly neurotic to demand that others treat you fairly; that kindness should be returned with kindness; and, that the world should be a comfortable, decent place to live. Affirming this bilge (nonsense) causes you to become depressed, hurt and even angry when things don't go the way you believe they should go. The rule of life is that unfair and unkind behavior occurs in response to your kindness. The faster you recognize that life happenings will probably always be that way, the healthier, non-depressed person you are.

Other-Pity is the third cause of depression. There's no denying the fact that there are millions of people who are suffering, troubled and unfortunate (especially those who have untimely passed away). Pitying these poor souls results in you causing yourself to become depressed in the same way as if you pitied or blamed yourself.

It makes no difference which of these three directions you take to instill depression, you are in emotional pain.

[Now it's time for you to learn how to edit yourself and purge self-destructive thoughts.] How do you stop neurotically blaming yourself? [This mental jailbreak is accomplished by **separating your behavior from you as a whole person.**] As a whole person, you can never be a *good* person or a *bad* person. **You** are only a person who does good things and bad things. Your actions and behaviors are only a part of you. **All of you** consists of all of your behaviors, both the goods and the bads. Since you are a mixture of good and bad actions, you can never be a worthwhile or worthless person. Confess/admit that you are wrong when you have committed something that you think is immoral or bad or needlessly painful to others. But, **stop right there and do nothing more.** This ends my recounting of Dr. Hauck's work. If I counted correctly: 421 words.

Upgrading your head with this refined mental landscape enables you to be free of upsetness about your behavior. Your adaptive thought goes like this: "My bad behavior **only proves** I am human. I'm not a bad person for acting poorly. I'm not a shit for acting shitily. Vaporize all self-blame!

Remind yourself ad nauseam that whenever you believe your behavior is undesirable, wrong or bad that it causes you to ***only evaluate your behavior!***

It's important to understand that nothing in life is awful, horrible, terrible, catastrophic or tragic. The worst that anything can be in life is bad, inconvenient, a pain-in-the-neck or a pain-in-the-ass!

So whenever you fail to obtain what you want, that causes you to think that it's ***only too bad*** and thus to ***only feel disappointed!***

Whenever you make a mistake, it causes you to think that the mistake only proves you are a fallible person. Now, you view your errors as a way to improve. When you act badly, you stubbornly refuse to damn yourself. Being treated unfairly by others, you now recognize it's their problem and not yours. While you do not like being treated unfairly, you refuse to put yourself down.

So far I've explained that **you feel the way you think.** So the cause of grief/depression (or any upsetness) is to identify the halitosis of the mind, aka, *stinking thinking* and replace these thoughts with adaptive, logical beliefs. There is another **proven mental secret to prevent your mind from turning to stone.** This second or alternative method is to just focus on those thoughts that enable you to feel how you want to feel being free of upsetness. This method indirectly attacks your self-defeating belief system.

Alternative Solution To Stress

To achieve the best (and fastest) results with this second method I call **Emotional Enhancement,** your thinking would best be done with your eyes closed. (You can implement either solution with your eyes open or closed. And, sometimes it isn't practical to have or possible for your eyes to be open). By closing your eyes you shut down one eighth of the body's ability to process information, thereby placing you in a maximum position to picture, visualize and imagine. This, in turn, allows you to enhance your focus on what **emotion(s)** you want to experience rather than the stressful feelings.

I think the best way for me to explicate this alternative method is to role play. So let's pretend you are the patient/client and I am the therapist. You have just become stressed out, depressed about something. This is what I'd say to you (which you can then subsequently reiterate to yourself).

"Now it's time for you to do some serious thinking. What are you going to think about? You're going to think about your desires. You're going to think about the changes in your life you have a full desire to make. Your thoughts are required to follow a particular and precise pattern. First of all the word 'will' is strictly to be avoided in your thought rehabilitative thought process. The word 'will' means something is going to happen in the future. But, you only function **now,** at this moment, in the present time! So all of your thoughts are to be couched in the present tense. Everything begins for you **now**, at this moment, and continues into the future.

There are two things for you to think about. The first are the events that you wish to create. Or those events that you wish to eliminate. The second is how do you **feel** participating in the new events? And, how do you **feel** not doing the things you used to do? **For you,** the second is equally important as the first. Since virtually everything you do in life is preceded by a thought, then you send your brain some messages by how you think. You see, your brain takes your thoughts, your messages, your directives, your commands, your suggestions and processes and programs those into your body. It's your mind that tells your brain what to do with your body. How you **think**, that's who you are! How you **think**, that's what you do! How you **think**, is how you **feel.**

Your brain processes and programs those thoughts at the very moment that you cause these thoughts to be delivered to your brain by how you **think**.

So now it's time for you to do some productive thinking and send your brain some messages. And, you know these messages are to be in the present tense. For you, everything begins **now** and continues into the future. Avoid using the word 'will' because 'will' means something is going to happen in the future. But, **you only function at this moment,** in the present time

So, if you want to be a certain kind of a person characteristically, personality-wise, you have to send your brain a message. This allows your brain to process and program those thoughts into your body causing you to become the sum total of your thoughts.

So, if you want to become the most relaxed person, the most comfortable person, the most contented person wherever you are and under any set of circumstances, you think like this. 'I am the most relaxed person wherever I go, under any and every set of circumstances. I am the most comfortable, the most pleasant, and the most peaceful in my mind and my whole body. 'Cause I'm the one in charge whatever I do. I control my thoughts. I definitely control my emotions, my feelings, my symptoms. That's me! I sure love who I am.'

So, if you want to be a compassionate and a caring person, then you think: 'I am compassionate and caring.

I'm comfortable and contented all the time. I am joyful and happy wherever I go, wherever I am, whether I'm alone or with others. That's me!'

You see, if you don't send your brain a message, the brain has nothing to process into your body. Nothing to create. The brain only follows two messages. To do something, or stop doing whatever it is doing. Either an inhibitory message or an excitatory message. To do or not to do. Your brain never follows a 'don't do message or 'I am not' message. Your brain creates, causes things to happen, or stops whatever was created.

Understand, you don't get out of a chair until **first you decide** to get out of a chair. You don't walk in any direction until **first you decide** what direction. How far. How fast. When to stop.

You see, it's always these messages by how you think that are processed within your body. And so, if you want to **be**, you tell yourself: 'I am.' **Not 'I will be.'** But, **'I am!'** 'I am the most comfortable, the most contented, the most pleasant, the most relaxed, the most satisfied, the most joyful and the happiest person whether I'm sitting in a chair at home, lying in a bed, whether I'm alone or with others.' It's your mind that tells your brain what to do to your body! You can choose. You can select. You can determine each and every thought. So you can be happy or joyful. Or, you can be depressed and down-in-the-dumps. **It's a choice!**

Once your choice is made and delivered to the brain, then the brain begins to process this particular choice of yours into your body.

So, if you are depressed, you're lonely, you're upset, think you are a failure, your brain has no choice but to process that thought (or those thoughts) into your body. If you want to be somebody **different**, then it's time for **you to think differently.** Thus, you have to send a **different message** for you brain to process and program. Your brain has no choice but to carry out every thought that you deliver. The more specific, the more detailed your thoughts are, the better results you're going to get.

Depression is a symptom, a feeling caused and created after you deliver a message to your brain. Messages like: 'I don't like it here. I'm lonely. I'm upset. I'm left alone. I can't get things done.' With those kind of messages, what do you expect your brain to do for you? Change your messages? Your brain never does that for you. Your brain only carries out the message by how you think!

So you can correctively think to yourself: 'I may have time on my hands, but I can find things to do. I can sit here and be joyful and happy.' If loneliness is a problem, go see your neighbor or go visit someone. Call someone on the telephone. Read. Do something to occupy your time. The point is, the **choice is yours!** It's always been yours.

If you think you **are, then you become that person!** Your thoughts can be: I'm contented sitting here by myself. I'm joyful and happy. I'm only sad not depressed. I'm compassionate and caring. 'Cause I'm the one in **control** of whatever I do. I'm **in charge** of how **I feel!** Life is pleasant. Life is wonderful, really is. Life is rewarding.' 'Cause life is what you make it just by how you think!

So what does it take? Just a thought. It's only a thought. It's always a thought. Be good and respectful to yourself. Love who you are.

Understand, there's no cell in your body that's **fear.** There's no cell in your body that's **anger or hate or loneliness or depression.** So what is depression and fear? It's your **perception (view)** of an event, a **thought.** How you **perceive** a situation to be. So anger, hate, loneliness and depression are simply and completely a product of **how you think!** Your thoughts are not anything material. Your thoughts are not part of your body. Your thoughts occupy no time, no space. And, therefore this depression can only be a product of how you think. Depression, in essence, you can't touch. You can't see a thought. You can't touch or feel with your hands the depression. They're in the image and likeness of each other. They don't exist until you cause it to be created. Created by how you think.

See, if you think to yourself, 'I'm happy and joyful', it may not be true at the time. But as soon as you deliver that message by how you think, then the brain has no choice but to make you happy and joyful **after** – you see it's always **after** – you deliver the message.

So what does it take? **Just a thought!** Well isn't that nice? No medication. No treatment. No surgery. Just a thought. But, it's only the thought! No pills! Change how you think. You change how you feel. "I am who?' 'I am not depressed.' No, **No, No!** The brain doesn't process a 'not' or 'don't do' message. The brain only creates, makes something happen. Give your brain something to do. Think: 'I am joyful. I am happy.' These are the opposite of being depressed. Or you might think you're only appropriately sad, sorrowful, or regretful. Also the opposite of being depressed is thinking: 'I'm comfortable and contented.' Create something by how you think. That's what you theoretically have to do. And, once you create the opposite (flip your own self-defeating suggestion), the depression leaves your body. These new, good messages push out the old messages right out of your body. Think of this process as sweating toxic messages through the pores of your body.

You can take this self-enhancement process one step further with thoughts like this: 'When I exercise, the exercise causes me to feel comfortable, contented and pleasant. When I walk, walking causes me to feel comfortable, pleasant, safe and satisfied.'

You see, you can create any symptom you want simply by how you think. It just takes a thought. Another example: 'When I read the paper, that causes me to feel wonderful, pleasant, knowledgeable and intelligent. That's me! And, I love who I am.' You'd better love who you (have true self-confidence)! You have the right to occupy your body. You have the right to use your body. You have the privilege to enjoy that body. It's all yours. So, why not treat that body of yours with dignity, with respect, with love and compassion? Why not!? That body is your most important possession. The most important thing you're going to own in your whole lifetime. Love who you are!

You and I and all of us, we are the sum total of our thoughts. That's who we are! So if you want to **be**, you have to send your brain a message like: 'I'm joyful and happy. Comfortable. Contented. Peaceful in mind and body. Secure in every respect. I am capable. I am successful. I am competent. And, I love who I am.'

Again, what does it take? Just a thought. It's only a thought. But, it's always a thought. Without the thought, your brain has nothing to process, to program into your body. Recognize, it's your mind that tells your brain what to do to your body. That leaves you **in charge. Leaves you in control** to choose and to select how you feel at any time in your life, and at any place in your life, under any set of circumstances and all the conditions you may be involved in. **You are the BOSS!** Be nice to yourself. Think well of yourself. That body is the most valuable thing you're going to own in your whole lifetime. You make that body comfortable, contented, peaceful, secure, joyful and happy, **just by how you think!"**

You probably noticed a fair amount of **repetition** in the above explanation of **emotional enhancement.** That was deliberate. Your mind, more accurately your subconscious mind, requires a reasonable amount of repetition in order to recognize that you mean business about incorporating some new data or removing old data. Repetition is an indisputable fact, established principle about human learning. Even the most intelligent among us requires some repetition, maybe less than a lot of others. We don't learn by osmosis.

This leads me to explain more completely how the human mind operates. We were made in two sections and put together. You got a left side and a right side. Put together, they make one body. You got a left and right part of your brain. Put together, they make one brain. And, you've got your mind in two parts. You've got a conscious and subconscious mind.

Your conscious mind is your thinking portion. That's what you do to analyze, analyzing incoming information, stimuli. And, this information you put into your brain (memory bank) for storage.. The other part, subconscious, is the functioning one. The subconscious reads what the conscious mind puts in and tells the brain what to do.

When you were born, the subconscious mind was the boss. It told your brain what to do. Your conscious mind, your reasoning ability was years away from being developed. As you began to grow, develop and learn and went to school, you began to educate your conscious mind so you could think. As your conscious mind became more educated and learned how to reason, it began to take control of the things you do and think about. (This process is called "reaching the age of reason", which usually occurs between the ages of 7 to 9 years.) Your subconscious mind then went down below – was relegated to a **sub** position. Thus, your subconscious mind became the **sub**ordinate part of the brain and body. The processes of closing your eyes, stopping and thinking, and repetition, as well as engaging in progressive relaxation brings your subconscious mind to the top – to the foremost. You make the subconscious the boss again. That enables you to work with your subconscious mind, which is always there to protect you – to get you to do the things that are beneficial. And, to keep you alive and keep you healthy, undisturbed by programming, advertising and everything else you want to avoid. So when you get yourself into a position where your subconscious mind is dominant, you're talking directly to your subconscious mind which is your protector, your guardian. This, then, is how you're able to wash away the programming that was done by the media, by certain people and so forth that tried to control you. You see, your subconscious mind is what's going to keep you healthy and strong. So your suggestions (affirmations) and messages are funneled into your brain thru the subconscious level. Your subconscious mind controls your brain which in turn controls every cell in your body. This condition where our subconscious mind is in the dominant position occurs naturally and briefly hundreds of times daily – but most people are unaware of this process. Daydreaming is a good example of this subconscious dominant position.

How To Put Your Subconscious Mind On Steroids

So, let me ask: do you want to accelerate your mental fitness? Yes, of course!!! Now I'm going to show you a technique that gives you weapons-grade *thought power.* Before I do that, I want to interject a certitude or naked truth about human behavior lurking in the background. Common sense dictates for most persons that our logical thinking process is disabled when we experience any kind of stress, emotional turmoil or upsetness. We then begin to think less rationally and more morbidly. This same common sense also commands the opposite: that a relaxed mind is optimally endowed to function unfettered with logic and reason. The **key word is: relaxed/ relaxation!** So this technique is termed **Progressive Relaxation.** So, once again, let's pretend I'm your therapist training/teaching you how to progressively relax you mind and body.

The vast majority of professionals who teach patients/clients progressive relaxation do so in the wrong direction. They start at the toes/feet and work up to the head. That just simply doesn't make any sense. Your brain/mind is in you head. So if you start at the source of your "aliveness" and relax that first the rest of the body falls into place pretty rapidly. Subsequently, you can achieve total relaxation in a matter of seconds. So here we go.

First get yourself in a comfortable position. Laying down on a bed, couch or the floor. Maybe in a recliner or some type of comfy chair. Could even be a hammock. Whatever you find is comfortable. Next, you close your eyes and keep them closed thru the entire process when you're doing this to yourself. Not here, because you have to read what I'm saying.

Now you direct your attention to your eyelids and your eye muscles. And, you relax your eyelids. You make your eyelids comfortably closed, pleasantly closed. Bring upon a feeling in your eyelids that, for you, is comfortable, restful and relaxing. So, please, be aware of what you are doing. Make those eyelids ever so limp...deeply relaxed.

And, now direct your attention to the forehead, area around your eyebrows. If you can picture and imagine that right smack in the center of your forehead, and just above the bridge of your nose, you got a dab or a spot of some creamy, fluffy lotion. Lotion that is soothing. Lotion that is comfortable. Lotion that feels pleasant. And, lotion that penetrates, sort of seeps into the pores of your skin. Imagine this lotion slowly begins to absorb and gather the warmth from your body. And, this lotion seems to get warm. And, now the lotion starts to gently glide and slide – kind of melt and spread – and gently flow across your forehead. Soothing and caressing. Penetrating in the tiny pores sending a feeling of comfort deep, deep into the forehead. Imagine this relaxation spreads all the way across your forehead and penetrates deep, deep into the forehead.

And, something soothing and comfortable and pleasant trickles from the forehead down over and across both of your temples. This feeling of relaxation settles in your cheeks. But seems to creep and spread throughout the cheek muscles, touching and causing the cheek muscles to relax. Now you take another moment...and you direct your attention to your cheeks. You make your cheek muscles ever so limp. I mean totally rested...deeply relaxed. If you like, feel the cheek muscles drooping, kind of hanging, sagging, trying to let go but still stuck there...

And, you find that each passing moment causes your cheek muscles and your eyelids and eye muscles to relax even progressively more.

So while your cheek muscles continue to relax all by themselves, imagine that some of this relaxation from your cheeks, seems to let go and starts to drain down and settle in the jaw muscles. But deep, deep into the jaw muscles. Imagine this relaxation begins to expand and spread from your jaw muscles over to your chin and then up to your lips. Touching and causing your lip muscles to relax...

But you take another moment now...and you focus your attention on your lips. And, come on, you make your lips nice and soft. Give your lips a pleasant feeling, a soothing sensation. Something comfortable and peaceful, yet deeply relaxing.

You see I know, I know when you relax your jaw muscles and your lips and mouth muscles, your lips have a tendency to part and separate as you allow this relaxation to penetrate deeper...and deeper, even deeper within.

Then, from the forehead, imagine something soothing and caressing and comfortable seems to kind of creep and spread and flow from the forehead up towards the top of the head. Soothing and caressing and penetrating and comforting all across the top of the head. Might even trickle down the sides of the head just above your ears.

Let this relaxation, this comfortable feeling continue to spread and flow down the back of your head. And, the feeling of deep relaxation seems to settle in the back of the neck.

And, then you imagine that this relaxation that **you just caused to be created**...seems to kind of drain down from the top of the head and forehead, slowly seep down from your eyelids, your cheeks, your lips, jaw muscles and chin, down thru the neck into the shoulders. And, as this relaxation touches the shoulders, it spreads and flows across your shoulders like a soothing sensation. A wave of relaxation touching and penetrating and resting not only the muscles in your shoulders, but comforting the nerves, tendons, the tissues. Caressing every cell, every gland, every tissue. Everything deep...deep in your shoulders. Imagine this relaxation spreads all the way across your shoulders.

And something soothing and comfortable and pleasant flows over the shoulders down both of your arms. That's over the skin and deep, deep inside your arms. Slowly, every slowly flowing downward touching and resting the muscles in your arms. Even comforting the nerves, the tendons, the tissues. Resting every cell, every gland, every fiber. Everything from the shoulders down, down both of your arms all the way to the elbows. Causes your arms now from shoulders to the elbows to go more relaxed and more comfortable and progressively more deeply relaxed.

But this relaxation continues to flow and spread past the elbows, again over the skin and deep, deep inside. Slowly flowing but touching and soothing and caressing, comforting and relaxing everything in its path.

And, this relaxation flows from the elbows down, down both of your arms all the way down to the wrists. Causing your arms now from the shoulders to the elbows to the wrists to go more rested, progressively more deeply relaxed.

And, then this relaxation continues to flow and spread past the wrists. Imagine something soothing flows from the wrists over the back of your hands. A pleasant sensation from the wrists into the palms of your hands. Then all this relaxation continues to flow past the knuckles into each and every one of your fingers all the way down to the fingertips. Causing your arms now from the shoulders to the elbows to the wrists to the fingertips to grow more rested, more comfortable and more deeply relaxed.

Now, from the shoulders, imagine something soothing and caressing, comfortable and pleasant, and peaceful and relaxing flows from the shoulders into the chest area, from the back of your shoulders down your back. Imagine your body being draped, draped in the most soothing sensation, the most pleasant feeling, the most peaceful. Thoroughly relaxing from the shoulders into the chest area. Spreads all the way across the chest, deep into the chest area. Might trickle down the sides of your body.

And, from the back of the shoulders, this relaxation slowly flows down touching and caressing and comforting everything from the back of the shoulders down, down, down your back to the lower back. And, this relaxation from the chest area flows into the stomach area. Then all of this relaxation seems to settle in your hips. Momentarily hesitates at the hips. But penetrates, comforts and relaxes all the muscles, the tissues. Every fiber, every gland, every nerve, everything deep, deep in the hips.

And then this relaxation slowly begins to flow from your hips down both of your legs past your knees, down to your lower legs into your feet and right to the ends of your toes.

At this point you can pickup your self-treatment from above where I started the explanation of the Emotional Enhancement method: "Now it's time for you to do some serious thinking." And/or you can employ the first method of disputing your self-sabotaging beliefs.

You could record yourself (or have someone else record) this progressive relaxation script including one of the above methods plus a second recording of the other method. Either one would be around 20 to 30 minutes maybe even less. You don't need to use my exact words. Put everything in your own words that are meaningful to you. Your recordings can be cassette tapes, CD's, or CD's via a computer. You can listen to them on whatever electronic device you want or download the recording to a I-pod. All of this won't take you much time to do. So, do yourself a favor and produce the recordings. You'll be ecstatic that you did and the results you generate!

You will only have to listen to the recording(s) a few times before relying solely upon yourself. I say a "few" because everyone's different in their learning abilities. You'll know what "few" means for you.

When you're ready to go- it- alone, guess what? You only need to do the progressive relaxation plus the adaptive thinking for a maximum of three (3) minutes or less. You can silently think a hell-of-a-lot faster that you can listen, speak or read. So with a little practice you can get yourself profoundly relaxed, as I said earlier, in a few seconds. And, you find you only need to get to your shoulders before your whole body is zonked out.

I practice these methods two to three times daily for about 1 to 2 minutes. Not so much for stress balancing (eliminating mental pollution) but prophylactically to keep myself stress free.

There is a third, corollary, technique that you can employ to correct adverse stress called **Rational-Emotive Imagery.** I will briefly describe it here.

First, allow (imagine) yourself to **feel** upset (anxious, depressed, or angry). Then change your emotion to one of concern but *not* stress by changing your thoughts/ideas about the circumstance. Practicing this fantasizing/visualization technique often is required until you get the results you're looking for. Dr. Albert Ellis (the inventor of REBT) acknowledged that visualization techniques combining imagining and thinking methods are the most effective Rational-Emotive Behavior Therapy techniques (***A Guide To Rational Living, 3rd Edition, 1997, Page 232.)*** I urge you to buy this book. Here's the website address: ***info @albertellis.org. Or Telephone Number (212) 535-0822.***

CHAPTER

THE CAUSES AND CURE OF EMOTIONAL TURMOIL

"Words are but pictures of our thoughts." John Dryden

AS NOTED IN the last chapter above, the basic cause of virtually all emotional turmoil is your thinking. More specifically unhelpful, illogical ideas. What I didn't illuminate, however, is what exactly constitutes illogical thinking.

Irrational beliefs are defined as ***demands*** or ***absolutes.*** We create demanding or absolutistic beliefs by the following six (6) verbs: have, must, ought, should, got and need. There are also five (5) other words (verbs) that mean the same as the have's, must's, ought's, should's, got's, and need's. These are: awful, terrible, horrible, catastrophe, and tragedy.

To believe that something is awful or terrible is tantamount to believing that *it shouldn't exist.* Believing that something is terrible or catastrophic is believing that it is more than 100% inconvenient. But nothing is more than 100% inconvenient. One hundred percent inconvenience, by definition, is death. The worst that anything can be is bad, inconvenient, or a pain-in-the-ass. When you define something as awful etc., you feel awful. So, virtually nothing in life can be awful, terrible, horrible, tragic, or catastrophic. So, the conclusion then, is that behind virtually every emotional upsetness, one of those verbs (shoulds/awfuls) is involved.

We develop illogical beliefs by taking a rational belief and stretching it to the extreme. Here's an example. 'I **want** to be loved.' Which is rational. And, then conclude: 'I therefore **should** be loved. Using the should's etc. renders the statement unprovable.. Demanding or commanding that a situation be different than it is, does not automatically make it happen, change or alter it. Reality is what it is! Reality often stinks! No matter what happens to us that we consider unpleasant, the fact remains that the undesirable event has taken place and that cannot be changed.

So, whenever you make yourself upset, you're only half wrong because you started off with a sane idea before you exploded that idea dogmatically.

Rational, self-actualizing beliefs express a wish, desire or preference. Negative sane beliefs create appropriate negative feelings such as: irritation, annoyance and frustration on the one hand. Sadness, sorrow and regret on the other hand..

Here's an example. Let's say it's raining outside. You **don't like** the rain because you'd rather have sunshine to sunbathe. Your rational belief could go like this (or something similar): "I don't like the fact that it is raining. With only that belief you would create the appropriate negative feeling of frustration, irritation, annoyance, displeasure or dislike.

By taking this rational idea to the extreme and saying/concluding: "It **should not** be raining because I want to sunbathe", you have ridiculously demanded that you **should have** what you want! The fact is that it is raining. Neither you nor I (nor anyone for that matter that I know of) can change that reality and stop the rain. No matter how different you **wish** reality to be, it undoubtedly is the way it is. And, there is no logical reason why reality **should ever be different!**

In the example I just cited, all you have to do is substitute the word "behavior" for rain and the same reasoning would apply to any human behavior.

Thus, no matter how you or another person behaves or acts, you would not be able to logically prove you or another **should** or **must behave differently.**

Reality is what it is. We have no godlike power that I know of to change reality. At best, we can only *attempt* to influence reality to change. Such as trying to appropriately influence someone to modify their behavior.

All nonsensical statements (using the shoulds etc.) have one thing in common: that a wrong has occurred and, therefore, **should not** occur. Condemning someone because they have behaved badly only results in you needlessly becoming stressed out. Think about it this way. Does a human being have the right, freedom, prerogative, choice to be wrong? Of course we do!!! If we do not have the right to be wrong, why then even be alive?! Aren't we all fallible, wrong-doing, mistake-makers? Who among us is perfect? Every time I tried to walk-on-water, I tripped on the waves.

So, not only do you have the right to be wrong, but to commit the same wrong act repeatedly. To say to another: "You should not be wrong."is the same as saying, "You should be right." Which is the same as saying: "You should be perfect." Since none of us can be perfect, isn't it kind of stupid behavior to demand that others act rightfully or not act wrongfully?

It is often true that you and others act poorly. It is not sane to conclude that any of us **should not behave badly.** That type of reasoning is called an overgeneralization.

Reiterating what I said earlier: we can neither be ***good persons*** or ***bad persons.*** We can neither be ***worthwhile*** or ***worthless.*** We can only be human, meaning an ongoing process constantly changing and consisting of a set of likes and a set of dislikes. Even our likes and dislikes change from time to time. It is foolish to rate ourselves as whole persons. It is quite logical and appropriate to rate our ***behavior*** as good or bad, right or wrong, moral or immoral. In this manner, you do not have to put yourself down for any act or behavior. Moreover, you then become a thoroughly **responsible** individual with a true sense of wrongdoing and accountability.

When you act humanly as in making an error or behaving poorly, you can then simply say to yourself: "I behaved badly but that doesn't make me a bad person. My bad act **only proves** I'm human! Now let's see if I can act less badly in the future." With this attitude, you are: (1) admitting your wrongness; (2) facing the reality or fact of your undesireable behavior; (3) **accepting yourself** as a fallible person; and (4) becoming **problem-solving** by resolving to try to do better in the future.

When you overgeneralize by downing yourself and viewing yourself as no good and worthless, you are problem-focused. And, additionally, you are insanely demanding that you **should not** act badly. This results in your becoming upset, having a poor self-concept. In turn, this places you in the self-defeating position of continuing to do the same wrong thing almost consistently. This self-destructive attitude gives rise to a corollary negative belief usually referred to as a **self-fulfilling prophecy.** That is, you begin to believe: "How can a worthless person do anything but immoral, bad acts? Therefore, I always act badly." Thus, you expect to fail or behave badly. With this self-expectation, you continually create needless failures and improper behaviors. So goes the vicious circle/cycle.

So what's the bottom line? This: **No one is condemnable or blameworthy for anything they do wrong including of course yourself!** Maintaining this belief places you in the position of practically never, or rarely, becoming upset.

A word of caution. I don't want to leave you with the impression that using the verbs have, must, ought, should, got, and need is always categorically wrong or irrational. Sometimes these verbs have a correct usage. This correct usage follows the logic: If X, then Y. For example: If I want to keep my job (X), then I have to (must, need etc.) show up and do the job (Y). In the alternative, you could preface the should etc verbs with the word "theoretically". Hence, "I theoretically should get to work on time." The statement, "I should get to work on time." Implies the word "theoretical". Only the person making the "should" etc. statement can corroborate their logic via how they feel at the time they verbalize their belief.

The same may be said for the verbs: awful, terrible, horrible, catastrophic,, and tragic. Some people use one or more of these words only to mean bad or undesirable. But also, they can use these same words to really mean illogically awful. They, in essence, use the same word(s) having two different meanings. In the end, again, only that person can verify what they meant by "awful" etc. by carefully identifying the accompanying emotion. With someone who is prone **not** to be very introspective, it's really mind boggling. For a therapist, faced with this type of patient/client as well as one who has dual usage "awfuls" etc. it's a toughy. I've been in that dilemma many times but fortunately was able to handle it, with some diligent work.

We live in a world of probability and chance where absolutes *apparently* do not exist. If I had said: "Absolutes do not exist." That would have been an illogical absolutistic statement. So the word "apparently" is a qualifier.

Rational-Emotive Behavior Therapy identifies 10 to 12 self-defeating beliefs that we humans have learned. These illogical ideas are the cause of our emotional upsetness. A detailed analysis of each and all of these irrational attitudes is contained in the book I mentioned above, ***A Guide To Rational Living***. I urge you to purchase this book. As I said earlier I am not going to expound in detail about REBT. That's why I want you to purchase this book. I am, however, going to summarize the key points of Rational-Emotive Behavior Therapy.

As we journey through life we are faced with only three (3) types of stimuli or categories of events. The first type is *our own behavior*. The second category is *others behavior*. The *world's behavior* represents the third classification.

Those three (3) types of stimuli actually are the three (3) basic problems of living for we humans no matter where we live on this earth or what language we speak. For we all make ourselves upset in the same way with the same self-sabotaging ideas and words.

The first problem of living for all of us is *condemning or blaming ourself* which harvests the irrational feelings of anxiety, worry, fear, lack of self-confidence, insecurity, inferiority, crippling self-doubt and depression.

The second problem in living for each of us is the flip side of the same coin: *condemning or blaming others*. That escorts the illogical feelings of anger, hostility, madness, rage, and resentment.

The third problem in living we all face is: *condemning or blaming the world or world/environmental conditions*, which initiates self-defeating enragement about world conditions.

So the key to wiping out stress is to doggedly refuse to blame yourself, others, or the world.

Actually, we can boil down these three problems of living to one single problem of human existence, which is: *acting like a frigging baby!* Because every time we blame ourself, we are whining and crying about our behavior. When we damn others, we are whining and crying about their behavior. And, when we condemn the word, we are whining and crying about world conditions. Thus, our goal would best be to refrain strenuously from behaving like a baby. To marshal your weapons-grade mental resources to disabuse yourself from whining/crying about your, others and the world's behavior. Put differently, to accept reality for what it is: just undesirable.

"The price of Greatness is responsibility."
England's most famous Prime Minister, Winston Churchill

Bits, Pieces and Gems about Humanness

Is life about comfort? Or is it about making a difference in spite of pain?

Pregnant Quotes:

"Success is getting what you want. Happiness is wanting what you get." - Dale Carnegie

"Courage is fear holding on a minute longer." U.S. Army Gen. George S. Patton

Friends, let me have the latitude to expound on Gen. Patton's perspicacity about *courage.* First let me note that General George S. Patton is considered by some to be the greatest, #1, worldwide military General of all time! He consistently ranks among the top ten military Generals in history. So he's no slouch when it come to intelligence.

Impactful quotes pack a lot of meaning with very few words. Almost always, these quotes require reading between the lines."

Courage, definitionally, is the attitude of facing and dealing with anything perceived as difficult, dangerous or painful as opposed to withdrawing from it. Courage is being brave or *fearless*. So what does Gen. Patton mean or imply when he says: "Courage is fear holding on a minute longer."? That you take your *fear* and transform it into the emotion of granite determination with action-oriented resolve to "deal with it." The *fear* withers and is replaced by productivity. Maybe good. Maybe bad. But productivity nonetheless. ***Courage***, my friends, is the key word. Courage is an emotional equilizer! Courage allows you to transform/convert your self-sabotaging emotions into adaptive feelings. More often than not self-defeating negative emotions are not stand-alone feelings. Anger often contains anxiety and even depression. Depression and grief have slices of anxiety. Inextricably interwoven into the fabric of fear are anxiety and depression, and sometimes even anger. Some psychological theorists have posited that *anxiety* is the only ball-buster negative emotion and that all others are derivatives. Bottom line: our emotions are more complex than we may realize.

Let me share with you a short story from one of my patient's. On a Sunday, almost exactly 90 days after his wife passed away, he was at a church service. He was standing for part of the service, and while doing so, he was experiencing raw grief with crocodile tears streaming down his face. Within moments, he felt a forceful and powerful pressure on his right shoulder as if someone had placed their hand there. He was compelled to turn around to see who it was. But, no one, yes no one, was there! What do you think? Was that God comforting him? Was that the Holy Spirit comforting him? Was that his deceased wife comforting him. Was it all of the above or some combination of these three that was comforting him? Maybe you think none of the above. Does any of us know the answer? That's why religion is called ***FAITH!*** (Trivia: there are 33, 909 denominations of Christianity worldwide). I can tell you with professional certainty it was not a hallucination!

What's important is what the outcome that "comforting hand" had. **COURAGE! C-O-U-R-A-G-E!!** He developed the ***courage*** to face his fear of being/living without his wife. The ***courage*** to accept the inevitable poignant reality of death. The ***courage*** to have self-compassion. The

courage to recognize that we come into this world alone; and we depart alone.

So, ladies and gentlemen, now it's your turn to let the anthem of ***COURAGE*** flow through your mind and body. Don't try. Just do! Your only other choice is emotional suicide!!

Being deficient/imperfect and possessing great limitations means we are all subject to most of the headaches (monumental pains-in-the-ass) that civilization doles out most generously to us all.

The **real cure** to human dysfunction is *ownership mentality.* Wherein you recognize that you and you alone are the owner/master/author/captain of your ship/destiny. It's really a beautiful thing that each of us is the sole *cause* and *cure* of emotional turmoil. If it were really true that others and the world made us upset we would be royally screwed and hopeless! We can control how we think. We can slay our false beliefs. We can eviscerate our bad thoughts. We can manage our emotions. But we have no power to control how others think or world conditions. Look into the mirror and you discover your own worst enemy: yourself! **"If you do not conquer self, you will be conquered by self."** ***Napoleon Hill***

Quoting Dr. Albert Ellis: "We teach people that they upset themselves. We can't change the past, so we change how people are thinking, feeling and behaving today." That concisely states the strategy and remedy to human dysfunction.

I and REBT are attempting to teach the concept to "accept the *inevitable* only when it has *inevitability.* Herein is where the philosophy of the **so-called** serenity prayer. Alcoholics Anonymous popularized this prayer but fails to provide the origin. Many think the source of this prayer came from the Theologian Reinhold Niebuhr and even some Oriental philosophers. Dr. Albert Ellis (since philosophy was his hobby) discovered that the original proponent of the serenity prayer was St. Francis. With REBT modification/reformulation this serenity prayer now reads: **"Let me now have the determination to change what I can change, the serenity to accept what I cannot, and the wisdom to know the difference between the two."** The real focus to control/overcome emotional dysfunction is to think in terms of self-management. Pay attention to what you can control rather than what you can't control.

We human beings consistently **fulfill the expectations that we have of ourselves.** Those who smoke cigarettes, think of themselves as "smokers. How do they then act? They smoke cigarettes. Overweight people think of themselves as fat and, thus, they overeat. Persons who do not act confidently believe that they are lacking in self-confidence. Colloquially this known as a **self-fulfilling prophecy!**

Insanity Cure

An important key to resolving emotional dysfunction is to *stop and think.* To closely examine your own lilliputian (small minded) thinking in an effort to convert illogic into logic.. This is a ubiquitous issue highlighted years ago by a famous person whose initials are: A.E. If you thought the "A" was for "Albert", you would be right. But, if you thought the "E" was for "Ellis", you would be wrong. The answer is below after the quote.

"**Insanity:** doing the same thing over and over again and expecting different results." Albert Einstein.

Many have heard this quote but didn't know where it came from. You would think mental health people would know the source. But, not so. They are just as ignorant. So, if you pass on this insanity definition, please acknowledge Albert Einstein as the author. Thank you!

In this context, I am reminded of another perspicacious observation of Albert Einstein. Namely, "Two things are infinite: the universe and human stupidity; and I'm not sure about the universe." Isn't this the core mission of self-help books and mental health professionals to enable us to behave less stupidly!?

It is a psychological/medical axiom that stress is a component in all disease whether a cold or cancer.

A brief on grief. Grief has no expiration date. Each of us is different and heals at different rates. What is true is that there is a direct correlation between the bond of the deceased and the surviving family member. In the case of a spouse, the stronger the marital bond, the more intense the loss and (usually) the greater the duration of the grief. The same might be said for other types of familial relationships. Spousal bonds, however, are a separate and different breed. In my own case, I thought nadir occurred for me the moment I realized my wife passed. But, I was so wrong! Rock bottom, the lowest/darkest point of my life, occurred later when I was facing the finality of death!! Rock bottom always looks very ugly, but that doesn't mean it's the end! The moral is do your very best to enjoy life, as hard as it might be, because life does have an expiration date!!!

Is This The Worst That Can Happen?

In the *Introduction*, I noted that I believed it was important for a mental health therapist/counselor (whenever possible) to be appropriately self-disclosing. A therapist's/counselor's self-revelation can accelerate a patient's/clients growth/recovery/improvement/healing/issue resolution. Why? Because the patient/client recognizes the therapist understands their dilemma, is compassionate and empathetic, and is providing a solution.

Hopefully my shared experience in losing my Soulmate wife of 51 years (such special relationships are in a league of their own) has been helpful to you by now. But, if you're still majorly heartbroken and in the throes of deep grief, I offer the following fodder for your mind.

Those who are grieving over the loss of a loved one are very prone to believing that their loss is the worst thing that can happen to them. For a period, I was no exception in having this belief.

So, now I want to help you "bring home the mental bacon" and nail-down this "worst case" problem. To close and lock the door; and put it behind you.

I recently found out about a woman who, in the Summer of 2015, first lost her military daughter to suicide. This daughter was deployed overseas in Spain. It took three (3) – count 'um 1...2...3 – days before her body was found! It cost this unfortunate mother $20,000.00 to get her daughter's body brought back home. And, NO, the US Government/ military did not provide any financial assistance.. Intensifying matters during this process, this mother discovered a voicemail message from her daughter saying that she "was in too much pain to go on." That was only the beginning of a brain-busting downhill slide for this woman/ mother.

Shortly thereafter, this same woman/mother faced the stinging loss of her son in a vehicular accident. His body was so mangled that he had to be cremated.

At this point, this mother was in the beginning stage of grieving over the loss of both a son and a daughter. "Unfuc---- shit like this just isn't supposed to happen!" Right? Then, BAM!, just like a powerful kick in the gut, this poor mother lost her father to pulmonary fibrosis. Get this: **all three of these deaths occurred in about a 6 week period of time!**

And, that's not all. If her children's and father's gut-churning and mind-warping losses weren't enough, here's what came next. Not too long after these 3 family members deaths, this mother's brother had to be hospitalized to undergo some serious major surgery.

As bad as this woman's plight was, it could even be worse. And that, my friends, is the moral: **things can always be worse than what you're going through!** So, no matter how down -in -the –dumps you're feeling, *courageously* remind yourself "it could be a hell-of-a-lot worse."

My friend and colleague of 50+ years (I noted in Chapter 1), Dr. Robert Matirko, ad libed this to one of his patient's: "Lose your head and your ass goes with it." In the words of the wise man, Eric Hofer: "The hardest arithmetic to master is that which enables us to count our blessings."

• •

Most people live stunted lives and are vexed with troubles they feel keenly. By "most", Dr. Albert Ellis concluded of the world's population a whopping 95% are psychotic, borderline psychotic or neurotic. So that leaves only 5% of the remaining populous that are considered "normal". A "normal" person is someone with minimal anxiety and minimal hostility.

CHAPTER

FALLOUT, FRACTURED FAMILIES, AND CONCLUDING REMARKS

THOSE OF YOU who have no living family members and have lost a loved one only have to deal with managing the grief of your loss.

For everyone else, there are a myriad of family members including in-laws that have to be dealt with. Family relationships are complicated and a mixed basket. The research indicates that it is very rare indeed for siblings to get along harmoniously. It's not all that common. In my own case, I and my siblings did not have to experience discord with the passing of our parents. We were the exception rather than the rule.

A mind-blowing 80% to 90% of family relationships among bereaved adult children are strained consequent to the loss of a parent. Sibling relationships following the death of a parent are somewhat equivocal. Notwithstanding, here is some of the fallout and fracturing that ensues following the passing of a parent:

1. Siblings/adult children's relationships grow strained and distant.
2. After a parental death, the sibling relationship dynamics are reactivated that date back to adolescent and young adult years.

3. As time elapses after a parental death, siblings grow less close and more distant. In other words, decrements in sibling bonds.
4. The death of a parent often brings about a lack of rationality, maturity, and reasonableness.
5. Parental loss can result in the eruption of family conflict and fighting worsening already existing emotional wounds.
6. Arguments over possessions can tear a family apart.
7. Severe rifts and distress are common among family members.
8. The death of a mother (who is the family kin-keeper) can reactivate childhood conflicts and sibling rivalry that developed earlier.
9. A multiplicity of problematic family relations emerges.
10. There can be disagreements about funeral arrangements including the obituary writing/publication along with the distribution of the deceased's property. These, in turn, bring about conflict among bereaved siblings.
11. Actual or perceived parental favoritism results in a lack of contact with siblings plus escalating rivalry.
12. Conflicts and resentment emerge when one sibling or other family member believes there is an unequal distribution of labor.
13. Sibling strife is a conflict that travels into adulthood and reactivated.
14. Sometimes what looks like an idyllic family relationship can turn sour either fairly soon or delayed down the road. But, occur, it will.
15. Latent jealousies and unresolved conflicts bubble to the surface.
16. Some siblings carry a sense of injustice.
17. In exceeding rare cases, parental death can bring about greater closeness of those remaining family members.
18. And, then there are survivors (frequently children) of the departed (frequently a mother) who selfishly want to pursue self-serving (often motivated by some type of guilt, remorse or some other perverse reason) behavior blatantly controverting the known and expressed wishes of the deceased.

19. Akrasia (the psychological term is *cognitive dissonance*). Behavior that is exemplified by a lack of self-control wherein someone acts badly in spite of better judgment – a weakness of will.

Nothing! Nothing can prepare you for the loss of a spouse (especially a soulmate) or parent or other significant other!!!

What's important is for you to care for yourself. Understand, it's your responsibility to manage you depression, anger, resentment and grief. Especially to forgive yourself if you have acted badly. The psychological results of bereavement attenuate over time as survivors adjust to loss. And for some, the time it takes to heal may be prolonged. It's not an easy process, but it can be conquered. No one said life would be easy, did they?

Forgiveness

The enormity and highly probable animosity that afflicts family members is a serious issue that begs for a resolution. There are two choices. The first is to do nothing and wallow in your emotional pain. That choice means you are authoring your own book *"The art of ruthlessly kicking my own ass."* Continuing to feel irate and angry (refusing to forgive) is time-consuming and energy-wasting. Moreover, you have to give yourself therapy for the duration of the hostility. Do you really need that result? Doesn't it make a lot more sense to just let-it-go and just feel annoyed at worst? You don't need to make someone else's problem your problem.

Forgiveness, however, does not mean that you have to maintain a relationship with one or more people. Not everything is fixable or easily remedied in family relationships. In theory fixability exists. But pragmatically it does not. For some people the resentments are just too deep a chasm to cross. Reconciliation is possible, but highly unlikely. Think of it this way. The relationship is just to **toxic** and is better left alone. Be respectful and minimize the time you spend, if any, with the toxic personality. I am reminded here of an interesting piece of research reported nationally by Fox TV News sometime during the month of April 2016. The one trait that was common among wealthy people versus the rest of the population is that the vast majority of wealthy people uniformly and consistently avoid **toxic personalities.** Why burden yourself with needless irritation when you don't have to? So, if it's desirable for you, act like your wealthy and avoid like-the-plague **toxic personalities!**

Closing Remarks

Succintly.

"It takes a great man to be a good listener." ***Calvin Coolidge.*** So if you got this far, I assume something I've said is helping you.

*"Life is a long lesson in **humility.**"* James M. Barrie

Horace: *"The pen is the tongue of the mind."*

You don't have to even know or like someone in order to be nice to them, including a complete stranger. In the words of Samuel Johnson: "Kindness is in our power, even when fondness is not.

And finally, the most important quote of all from the inventor of Rational Emotive Behavior Therapy and the greatest Psychologist of all time. *"Life as we say in REBT, is frequently spelled **H-A-S-S-L-E.** A good deal of it, with thought and effort, you can greatly improve. Not all! Not completely."* ***Dr. Albert Ellis.***

EPILOGUE

"Thank you God for this good life and forgiveness if we do not love enough."
Garrison Keillor

I am eternally grateful and privileged to have had 51 years with my Soulmate Wife, Sylvia!!!

By my own self-appointed power I am hereby inducting my wife, Sylvia, as the first inductee into the World's Women's Hall-Of-Fame!!!

I thank God((even though it doesn't quite cover it) that He gave me Sylvia to be my Wife!!!!!!

LaughLogue

I thought it would be both incongruous and insensitive to end this book on a doom and gloom note. Not to mention depressive mental imprisonment.

Humor mitigates the overseriousness we humans are prone to develop. Besides, maybe you could call it confetti for the mind. Plus customer satisfaction is paramount. Don't you agree?

This tidbit, I'd like to share with you.

So hang on tight and laugh-your-ass off!!!

DRINKING GIN

A new cleric at his first Service became so anxious he was almost speechless.

Following the Service he queried the senior priest how he had done.

The head priest said, "At the time I get concerned over becoming anxious at

the rostrum, I place a glass of gin adjacent to the water glass.

If I start to get anxious, I take a sip."

So the next Sunday he heeded the Monsignor's suggestion.

At the start of his sermon, he became anxious and took a sip.

He then spoke very fluidly.

When he got back to his office after Mass,

he discovered a note on his door.

1) Sip the gin, don't gulp.

2) There are 10 commandments, not 12.

3) There are 12 disciples not 10

4) Jesus was consecrated, not constipated.

5) Jacob gambled his donkey, he did not bet his ass.

6) We do not refer to Jesus Christ as the late J.C.

7) The Father, Son, and Holy Ghost are not called Papa, Junior and the Spook.

8) David killed Goliath; he did not kick the shit out of him.

9) When David was struck by a rock, he fell off his donkey. Don't say he was stoned off his ass.

10) We do not call the cross the "Big T."

11) When Jesus broke bread at the Last Supper he said, "Take this and eat it for this is my body." He did not say "Eat me."

12) The Virgin Mary is not called "Mary with the Cherry."

13) The proper grace before a meal is not: Rub-A-dub-dub thanks for the grub, Yeah God.

14) Next Sunday there will be a taffy pulling contest at St. Peter's not a peter pulling contest at St. Taffy's.

How 'bout you pass on this good crap to someone you know requires a bit of help!?
Show some ***kindness!***

"Who sows virtue, reaps honor." Leonardo da Vinci

May God Bless you with a prosperous life! Memorial Day, May 30, 2016.

Printed in the United States
By Bookmasters